EATING DISORDERS

EATING DISORDERS
THE PATH TO RECOVERY

Dr Kate Middleton

LION

A Lion Book
an imprint of
Lion Hudson plc
Wilkinson House, Jordan Hill Road,
Oxford OX2 8DR, England
www.lionhudson.com
ISBN 978 0 7459 5278 9

First edition 2007
10 9 8 7 6 5 4 3 2

Acknowledgments
The publisher would like to thank Anorexia & Bulimia Care
and the individuals concerned for permission to reproduce
personal stories in this book. All publishing rights in the
stories are retained by Anorexia & Bulimia Care.

The text paper used in this book has been made from wood
independently certified as having come from sustainable forests.

A catalogue record for this book is available
from the British Library

Typeset in 11/13 IowanOldStyle BT
Printed and bound in Great Britain
by JF Print Ltd., Sparkford, Somerset

Contents

Introduction

There are a lot of reasons why you may have bought this book. Maybe you are struggling against an eating disorder yourself. Or you might be supporting someone who is. You may be working in an environment where you know several people at risk of eating disorders. Or perhaps you have concerns about someone you care about and want to learn more.

Whoever you are I want to reassure you of two things. First of all, I want you to know that it *is* possible to recover from eating disorders. Recovery is a really difficult subject for those suffering (more about this later in the book), but true recovery is about being happy – with yourself, with what you weigh and with your life. And this is possible. Working towards recovery is not easy though. It takes courage and determination in equal measure. For many it is a leap of faith: of starting to dare to believe they are someone worth loving and worth caring for.

In my work I have had the privilege of getting to know many people who have been fighting eating disorders. Without exception they are remarkable and wonderful people. So here is my second reassurance: those fighting an eating disorder are so much more than just their eating disorder. They are individuals, unique and wonderfully made, with individual skills, passions, desires and talents. This book is dedicated to all of them. It is my hope that through reading this, they might be able to start to take that leap of faith.

How to read this book

The book is split into four sections. Feel free to start with any section, as some will be more useful to certain readers than others.

Part 1 gives the facts about eating disorders. It covers the definitions and the physical and medical risks involved, and it looks at the cycles of behaviour that make up eating disorders. It also looks at some of the common factors that can contribute to eating disorders. Finally, and perhaps most importantly, it includes a section for sufferers who are trying to decide where they want to go next with their eating disorder. So if you are being nagged by other people to 'do something' about your eating problems but are not sure if you want to stop, or if you are thinking about recovery but aren't sure if you want to start, this is the section for you.

Part 2 looks at some of the psychology behind eating disorders and some of the common 'bad guys' that you might have heard about in relation to eating disorders. So, common personality factors, thinking styles or emotions that might be a part of the problem are all discussed here – along with some practical ideas to help you to deal with them.

Part 3 focuses on the issue of recovery from eating disorders: what it is, whether it is possible and how to move towards it. It also looks at the question of treatment and how to handle some of the difficult stages you might be facing, such as waiting lists, seeing your GP or undergoing in-patient treatment.

Finally, Part 4 is written specifically for parents. Eating disorders are becoming more and more common in younger children, which means that many parents are having to face the challenge of how to deal with their child's illness. This section answers some of the common questions from parents, and contains contributions from a parent who has been on this journey.

This is not a book written from theory. It is based on the experiences of many people who have struggled with eating disorders and battled along the road to recovery, and it could not have been written without them. My thanks to everyone who has shared their journey with me. It has been a privilege.

Part 1

Making a start

What are eating disorders and do you want to recover?

1 What are eating disorders?

Whoever you are, and whatever your reasons for buying this book, we are meeting here on this page because you have some kind of interest in eating disorders. If you read newspapers and magazines regularly, you will probably have come across the names of many different 'eating disorders'. Some of these you might know a lot about; others may be new to you. In this chapter I want to make sure we have the same understanding of what eating disorders are and what I mean by all the terms and jargon I use.

Most eating disorders come from the same basic root belief. Someone who is struggling with difficult thoughts, experiences, feelings or memories comes to believe that things would be different if they were thinner. This may show itself as a hatred of their own body – a conviction that they are fat and disgusting. Or it may simply be a drive to be thinner. Some sufferers start out genuinely overweight. Others simply think they are, or may have been told that they need to lose weight, for example through bullying or teasing. Whatever the reason, they come to place their hopes and aims on that one thing: in order to change their life they need to be thinner. An eating disorder develops because someone believes that losing weight will help them to cope with whatever life is throwing at them.

What comes next for sufferers is a resolve to change what they eat, and often to exercise more. It is a common myth (among sufferers as well as other people) that only those with anorexia restrict what they eat. That's not true though – most people with eating problems *aim* to restrict their food and set themselves strict diet plans. How well they manage to stick to this we will think about in a moment, but at this stage it is all about setting those plans. Most sufferers could give you a list of foods in their head that are 'forbidden' or 'bad'. They will also probably have 'good' foods which they allow themselves to eat, although some people simply aim to eat as little as possible, or even to fast for a period of time.

The third stage in developing an eating disorder is the one in which sufferers start to split into the different kinds of eating disorder, such as anorexia and bulimia. This is because what happens next depends on lots of things, including personality and practical issues such as whether or not it is possible to skip meals.

One group of people manage to stick resolutely to their diet plan. They restrict their eating severely, often cutting down more and more as time goes on – adding foods to their 'forbidden' list, counting calories or fat grams obsessively, and always compulsively chasing the control they long for. These people are those suffering from **anorexia nervosa**. The term 'anorexia' actually means a loss of appetite, whereas the 'nervosa' clarifies that this is something to do with the sufferer's mind. However, this is a bit misleading because in fact people with anorexia do not lose their appetite. Once they have suffered for a long time many do become so separated from the normal urges to eat that they no longer feel the sensation we would call hunger, but what causes them to stop eating is a tremendous act of will and self-control. Then, as the illness continues, the drive to keep restricting food starts to come from the fear of what will happen if they do allow themselves to eat.

People who suffer from anorexia lose dramatic amounts of weight. This can happen very quickly, or relatively gradually. Of course, if someone was overweight to begin with, this can take some time to show, so not all sufferers are very underweight. But one of the biggest risks of anorexia is the physical impact of someone effectively starving themselves over a long period of time.

However, it is a misconception that sufferers never eat. Very few manage to keep up the control all the time and most will eat sometimes. For some this loss of control may even trigger cycles of bingeing and purging, like those you will see in bulimia. But, overall, sufferers eat less than they need to, and so continue to lose weight.

Meanwhile, a key feature of anorexia is that although sufferers are underweight or losing weight, they do not see themselves as thin. In fact, many persist in thinking they are fat, even when their life is at risk because they are *so* thin. This, of course, is because being thinner does not actually make them feel better or solve the problems they are struggling with, so they continue to feel that they need to lose weight and be thinner. This is one of the things that make anorexia such a dangerous condition.

A second group of people, meanwhile, start off with very similar aims to those with anorexia, but practical things about their lives (for example, if they are living at home and cannot avoid meals) or their personalities mean that there are regular times when their control breaks down and they eat. These people struggle with bulimia nervosa or binge-eating disorder. During these times they typically start to eat the foods they had originally forbidden themselves – all those things on that list. Putting a food on a 'forbidden' list often means you immediately start to crave it, so when these people break down and allow themselves to eat, they tend to overeat and binge on large quantities of these foods. Binges tend to develop and worsen over time, and usually happen in secret. Some people will plan specifically for a binge. They feel a terrifying sense of being out of control, and may eat things they would never normally consider, such as uncooked food, food that does not belong to them or even dog or cat food. Binges are very frightening because they represent the thing the sufferer most wants to avoid.

People with **binge-eating disorder** live their lives struggling with episodes of binge-eating. They hate themselves and their weight, and are usually overweight or obese. Often they have been on every diet around and swing from one eating plan to another, but each time they are doomed to failure because their control eventually breaks down and another binge starts. Binges can be triggered by certain feelings and many sufferers would describe them as episodes of 'comfort eating'. They may talk about their lack of self-control and even joke about it, but underneath it is anything but a joke.

Additionally, there are those who struggle with **bulimia nervosa**. The term 'bulimia' describes someone who eats 'like an ox', and this relates to the binge-eating part of the disorder. People who suffer with bulimia develop a fourth stage of this vicious eating and dieting cycle. After a binge, seized with terror, regret and frustration at what they have done and desperate to avoid putting on weight, they begin to do something to purge what they have eaten. What they do varies, but can include things such as making themselves sick, taking laxatives or excessive exercise. They think that the purging makes things better, but in fact it makes the bingeing worse because swallowing food is no longer the 'point of no return' of eating. Now they have something they believe will stop them putting on weight when they binge-eat, so the binges tend to become more frequent and worse, involving more and more food. Some people binge and purge several times a day. Others lurch between bingeing and purging, and then aim to fast for several days in a desperate attempt to stop what they are doing.

People suffering with bulimia are usually convinced they are overweight and hate their appearance. However, in spite of feeling so dissatisfied, most are actually at or near normal weight. You cannot tell if someone has bulimia just by looking at them. Bulimia often carries on for years in secret without even close family knowing anything about it. Sufferers endure a regular cycle of difficult and painful feelings as they struggle with the triggers for and the consequences of binges. Very often they will try to stop bingeing – most hate themselves for doing it and feel very ashamed of what they do. But in their effort to stop, they actually set themselves up to fail, developing a new resolve to restrict their eating and therefore starting the whole cycle again.

What I have just described are the three main eating disorders. Of course, there are many variations of these three diagnostic terms, and often people do not fit one or another precisely. Add to this the fact that doctors and psychologists have specific criteria that someone has to meet to be diagnosed with a specific eating disorder, and you can understand why another disorder is commonly diagnosed: something called **EDNOS**. This means Eating Disorder Not Otherwise Specified, and is used when someone is plainly suffering with an eating disorder, but for one reason or another doesn't quite fit the criteria for anorexia, bulimia or binge-eating disorder. Perhaps they have anorexia, but have not yet lost enough weight to be clinically underweight. Or perhaps they are a man, or a younger girl, and so do not meet one of the criteria for anorexia, which is that a sufferer's periods have stopped (something called **amenorrhoea**). Or maybe they are struggling with bingeing and purging, but it is not yet occurring often enough to be diagnosed as bulimia (the criteria require someone to binge and purge at least twice a week for a minimum of three months).

Some common questions – and answers

My friends/family/teachers say they think I am anorexic, but I am not thin. Could I be fat and still be anorexic?

This is a really common question. In fact if I had a pound for every person who has said this to me I would be able to fund eating disorders charities for a very long time. A minority of sufferers will admit they are thin and want to be thinner, but this is unusual. One of the main symptoms of anorexia is that the person suffering thinks they are fat, even though they are not. So almost all sufferers feel this way. In fact it is the most common reason people will not go to the doctor: 'I am not thin enough to be anorexic, so if I go they will just laugh at me.' 'I can't be anorexic,' they say. 'I am not thin enough.' Or, 'The other people in the clinic were obviously anorexic because they were thin, but I bet everyone wondered what I was doing there.' Some people are amazed when they see anorexia down on their notes because they think they are enormously fat. One of the cruellest things about anorexia is that people spend all their time and energy and put themselves through real misery and pain trying to become thin, but when they really are thin they are never able to see that or get anything positive from it.

'Ah yes,' I can hear you thinking, 'that is true for lots of people, but not for me – I really am fat.' Don't let the eating disorder deceive you. It is hard to accept that these things are happening to you, and realizing that your own perception of yourself is wrong is very difficult. But do not let this stop you from winning your life back from anorexia. If your friends and family say you are thin, why not find out what they are basing this on? If they have some good evidence – maybe the size of clothes you wear, your weight, BMI (see page 28) or something else – maybe you should look at the possibility that you, like hundreds of thousands of others in the same position, are actually much thinner than you realize.

Of course, it is important to mention that some people do start off overweight when they develop anorexia. It can develop from other eating problems such as binge-eating disorder or bulimia and can also follow on from a diet that starts to go too far. So it may be that you are right and you are not actually underweight... yet. However, if your family and friends are saying this to you, then there must be something you are doing that makes them worry about you. Be honest with yourself – do you have any of the features of the eating disorders I have talked about? Eating disorders in general – and anorexia in particular – can be dangerous even before you get very thin, so if you are struggling with your eating you need to get some help before it becomes too serious. Even if your weight is still OK, if you have been losing weight very fast, or have been eating poorly for a long time, you might be at some physical or medical risk and certainly you might be struggling with an eating disorder. The sooner you get help and treatment the better, as it gets harder to break free from eating disorders the longer they go on. If you wait until you are very thin you may find control is taken from you as your physical health becomes critical. Take the time now to make some decisions about your future before the number of choices you have starts to dwindle.

All my friends make themselves sick after they have eaten too much, so it can't be that bad. Is it really an eating disorder?

It is true that things such as making yourself sick, fasting and even taking diet pills or laxatives are becoming much more common. Some studies suggest that over half of teenage girls and lots of boys regularly try these things, all in an attempt to control their weight. Most of these people will probably not develop a clinical eating disorder (that is, one which significantly disrupts their life, health or the way they feel). Many may dabble in some sort of purging from time to time and find that as they grow up they stop doing it. These people are still at some risk because none of these behaviours is risk free (see Chapter 2). However, if you are vulnerable to an eating disorder – perhaps if you are struggling with some of the things mentioned in Part 2 of this book – or if you are having to deal with abuse or traumatic events in your life, then you may find that they become more of a problem and develop into the kinds of vicious cycle I have mentioned above. If your eating (or not eating) is part of a cycle that includes times when you feel really low, depressed or desperate, then this is a sign that you need to get some help. You do not need to suffer like this, and the eating/dieting will only make things worse.

I went to the doctor and tried to explain what was going on, but s/he says I am just going through a difficult time/all teenagers feel like this/I should just try to stop worrying about what I eat/ I should just go home and eat a Mars bar.

All of the above comments are real examples I have heard from people who were suffering with a very real, and often serious, eating disorder. Diagnosing eating disorders is not easy, and many sufferers find it hard to be honest with doctors and tell them everything that is going on. Many doctors have received very little training in eating disorders and some studies show that they can find it hard to pick up on the subtle hints that patients will drop to try to let them know what is happening. Others simply don't understand eating disorders and will make what they think are helpful comments in an attempt to help. Although GPs are told they need to recognize eating disorders as early as possible, many find this difficult and, knowing that there are often long waiting lists for treatment, they take a 'wait and see' approach.

However, it is important that you get the help and treatment you need to overcome your eating disorder, and if you have just taken the brave step of telling your GP, responses like this can be devastating. Don't give up. If you need more support, call one of the helplines mentioned at the end of this book or think about taking a friend or relative with you to another appointment. If there is a different doctor you can see, give that a try, as GPs will vary in their approach and experience to eating disorders. Most of all, do not be swayed by the doctor's failure to recognize your symptoms. As I have already said, if your eating (or not eating) is part of a cycle that includes times when you feel really low, depressed or desperate, then this is a sign that you need to get some help. Have a look at Chapter 11, which gives some further tips for approaching GPs and getting help.

2 The physical and psychological effects of eating disorders

Eating disorders have their root in a desire to lose weight and be thinner, leading people into attempts to control their eating in some way, generally by restricting what they eat – or what most people would call 'going on a diet'. For some people this becomes the main focus of their eating disorder, and that restriction of their eating leads them to lose weight dramatically. For others, the breakdown of this strict resolve triggers the start of binge cycles, which may or may not then be followed by the development of some method of purging the food eaten. All of these three features of eating disorders have a physical impact on the body.

It is very important to be aware of the way eating disorders affect the body, for two main reasons. The first is perhaps the more obvious and the one that you will hear and read about most often: some of these behaviours carry a potentially very serious threat to health. People who are caught in cycles of certain kinds of behaviour can therefore be at very real risk of suffering some serious illness or even losing their lives as a result of what they are doing. They may not appear that ill – in fact they may outwardly seem quite healthy, fit and active. But inside, their bodies may be struggling to cope. The second reason is that many of the effects of starvation and food restriction actually trigger impulses and mechanisms in the body that may produce some of the behaviours that people struggling with eating disorders find the most alarming.

19

This chapter aims to look at the physical and psychological effects of eating disorders. First let us look at what happens to your mind and body if you go on too strict a diet. Then we will look at some of the physical impacts eating disorders can have on your body. This will include the risks of starvation and those that can be caused by purging, as well as thinking about obesity and the impact of long-term unhealthy eating.

What happens to the way you think when you restrict your diet?

One thing people suffering from eating disorders tend to overlook is the fact that what they are often doing is pushing their body into a state of apparent famine or starvation. As far as their body is concerned, suddenly the amount of food available has got worryingly low – far lower than the amount it needs to keep functioning. Of course, that is the idea: to get the body to use its reserves and therefore to lose weight. Almost everyone who develops an eating disorder will at some stage put themselves on a very strict diet.

There are some very interesting studies that look at what exactly happens to the body (and mind) when it enters a period of starvation. Our bodies and brains are programmed to try to survive, and some of those survival strategies are triggered very quickly if we go on too strict a diet.

One of the most well-known studies was conducted in the 1950s by a group of specialists led by Dr Ancel Keys.[1] The study looked at a group of men, who were screened for all kinds of physical and psychological abnormalities before the study began. They were then monitored for three months while they ate normally, before spending six months on a very strict diet that amounted to about half of their normal

[1] A. Keys et al., *The Biology of Human Starvation*, Vols 1 and 2, Minneapolis, MN: University of Minnesota Press, 1950.

food intake. Then finally they were monitored during three months of re-feeding. This study therefore theoretically allows us to see what impact this kind of restriction on diet has outside of what occurs when such dieting happens as part of an eating disorder. It is worth remembering that the diet these men were on – at about half of their normal food intake – was nothing like as severe as that which most of those struggling with eating disorders will aim for.

What happened to these men was striking. There were quite dramatic changes in eating habits, social attitudes, relationships and exercise patterns, many of them similar to the kinds of things we see happening in those who have eating disorders. Here are some quotes from Dr Keys' study – first of all from the restricted-diet phase.

About how they ate:

The subjects were often caught between conflicting desires to gulp their food down ravenously and consume it slowly so the taste and odour of each morsel would be fully appreciated. Towards the end of starvation some of the men would dawdle for almost two hours over a meal which previously they would have consumed in a matter of minutes.

About some unusual eating habits that developed:

The consumption of coffee and tea increased so dramatically that the men had to be limited to 9 cups per day. Similarly gum chewing had to be limited after it was discovered that one man was chewing as many as 40 packages a day.

About some social and behavioural changes:

Social initiative especially and sociability in general underwent a remarkable change. The men became reluctant to make decisions and to participate in group activities.

About changes to exercise attitudes:

Some men exercised deliberately at times. Some of them attempted to lose weight by driving themselves through periods of excessive expenditure of energy.

The impact of starvation continued when subjects were then allowed to eat an unrestricted diet in the third phase of the study. Many seemed to struggle with an uncontrollable urge to eat, and there were frequent reports of them losing control and experiencing binges that will sound very familiar to anyone who has suffered cycles of binge-eating as part of their eating disorder:

[One subject] suffered a complete loss of will-power and ate several cookies, a sack of popcorn and two overripe bananas before he could 'regain control' of himself. He immediately suffered a severe emotional upset, with nausea, and upon returning to the laboratory he vomited. He was self-deprecatory, expressing disgust and criticism.

One of the subjects ate immense meals (a daily estimate of 5–6 thousand calories) and yet started 'snacking' an hour after he finished a meal.

Subject no. 20 stuffs himself until he is bursting at the seams, to the point of nearly being sick, and still feels hungry; no. 120 reported that he had to discipline himself from eating so much as to become ill; and no. 30 had so little control over the mechanics of 'piling it in' that he simply had to stay away from food.

What is clear from these studies is that the act of placing yourself on a severely restricted diet in itself triggers some mechanisms that produce the behaviours most frightening to those fighting eating disorders. Certainly various other studies looking into this conclude that many of the features sufferers are most distressed by may have their root in the very restricted diets that many have been on. Things like the strong, sometimes uncontrollable, urge to eat may in fact be a side-effect of the body's response to starvation.

Remember, the men in these studies were psychologically and physically normal. A very common fear among those with eating disorders is that there is something basically wrong with them which means they will never be able to eat normally or cope with normal (unrestricted) eating. But this research shows us that the things that lead people to fear this are actually symptoms *any* normal person would encounter after a period of severely restricted eating.

So what does this mean for you if you are looking to recover from an eating disorder? Perhaps the most important message is that the urge you feel to restrict your food is probably itself causing the thing you fear the most: that urge to lose control and eat. People who have recovered from eating disorders confirm that this urge diminishes once a normal diet pattern is reintroduced. However, when someone who has been struggling with anorexia begins to eat again, it is a good idea in the early stages for someone else to help them to keep control of what they eat – so that they do not need to fear that natural urge to re-feed the body and replenish lost stores. Whether it is a GP monitoring weight gain or a friend or family member helping to plan and prepare meals, this support can be invaluable.

The really important lesson from this research is that a period of restriction leaves you at risk of experiencing binge-eating and a loss of control. Combine this normal reaction to starvation with the fear and anxiety an eating disorder brings and you have the recipe for a nasty vicious cycle: people restrict their diet and therefore set themselves up to risk a binge, then let down their control and experience that binge, then react to this in fear, terror and shame (even though what happened is just a normal human reaction to starvation), and go back onto that severely restricted diet, setting themselves up for the next binge…

This cycle is often the one that keeps eating disorders like bulimia and binge-eating disorder going. It can also lead people who have come out of a long period of restriction in anorexia – but have not had help to deal with the problems that underlie it – to swing from one eating disorder to another. If they are not given support, this period of loss of control and eating can be mistaken for recovery, and they then slip into a cycle of binge-eating and purging which can continue for years. If this is what has happened to you, please don't despair. You have become caught up in part by the way your body reacted to that initial period of starvation and then by your own fear. But it is possible to get out of this cycle.

What are the physical 'side-effects' of starvation?

Of course, starvation, or a period of time when you are undereating and therefore losing weight, has more than just psychological effects. The body is very like a car in that it requires constantly topping up with fuel to keep it going. This fuel provides energy so that muscle cells can keep contracting, nerves can keep firing and the brain can keep thinking. When the food you eat is not enough, you have to break down stores instead. Once there are insufficient stores, your body starts to use the only other source it has: the muscles and some organs such as the liver and kidneys. Therefore if you lose too much weight your body will start to break itself down in order to try to preserve the essential functions.

Obviously this brings with it a few problems, and I have called them side-effects because they are probably not something you ever intended to happen. If you carry on undereating too long, these organs start to struggle and you can develop kidney and liver problems. But perhaps most serious is the impact on the heart. The heart is basically one big muscle, contracting and sending blood all around the body. This muscle, just like any other, is broken down as your body looks for energy. This means that if your weight falls too low, your heart gets weaker and weaker as the muscle is broken down.

You might experience this in a variety of ways: your circulation is not as good as it was, meaning your fingers and toes get very cold and even sometimes go blue or white. Blood pressure starts to fall very low as well, so you might notice that when you stand up you feel very faint as your heart struggles to make the adjustment and pump the blood up that extra bit of height. Your pulse will also start to slow. Although it will still get faster when you exercise, when you are resting it might go as low as fifty beats per minute. All of these are serious signs that your heart is struggling and you need to get checked out by a doctor.

Undereating for a long period of time denies your body not just the energy but also the building blocks it needs for various essential parts. Your body cannot make everything it needs to work efficiently and healthily, so you have to get some of this from food. There are lots of essential nutrients, vitamins and minerals that your body cannot produce, and the longer your diet is poor, the more you risk developing a real deficiency in one of these. This can happen even if your weight is OK, for example if you have not yet lost that much weight but are eating very poorly, or if you eat enough to stay at a roughly normal weight but eat a very limited diet. It can even happen if you overeat and so are gaining weight, but your diet omits certain foods.

Although there are lots of different deficiencies that you might risk, these are perhaps the three most significant:

1. ANAEMIA

As your heart pumps the blood around your body the blood cells are bumped around in the blood vessels a bit like a car making a bad journey on a busy motorway. Because of this daily wear and tear they need to be regularly replaced, and for this your body needs new supplies – of iron and other things. Women in particular need plenty of iron because they lose red blood cells every month when they have their period. The main job of the red blood cells is to carry oxygen to the cells, and iron is essential for this. If you are anaemic, therefore, the symptoms you experience (including feeling tired, lethargic, breathless and even dizzy) are caused by your body being short of oxygen.

2. INFERTILITY

For women who are struggling with eating disorders, this is probably one of the main worries. The time when your ovaries mature in puberty, and your periods start, is determined in part by the levels of fat in your body. In basic terms, if you have enough fat supplies to be able to support a pregnancy, your ovaries mature accordingly. Therefore, if you become too thin – or more importantly if your fat levels fall too low (which can also happen through over-exercise or extreme sports training) – your ovaries can react, and return to their immature state. Ovulation stops and along with it your periods. Many women with eating disorders find their periods stop for many months or even years, and of course in this time you will be very unlikely to fall pregnant (though there is no guarantee, as you never know when you might ovulate, so you shouldn't rely on this). The good news is that for the vast majority of women, periods restart once weight (and body fat levels) comes back into the healthy range.

3. OSTEOPOROSIS

This is perhaps the problem that women with eating disorders should be particularly concerned about, but the reality is that many do not think about it at all. Osteoporosis is caused by an imbalance between the cells that make new bone and the cells that harvest old bone, meaning that bones become fragile and weak. If your diet is low in calcium you are at risk of osteoporosis, whether you are a man or a woman. Women are at particular risk because the speed at which bone is lost is regulated by oestrogen. If your periods stop because of your eating disorder, then your oestrogen levels will fall and your risk of osteoporosis increases. Adolescence is also a crucial time because this is when bone is laid down, and the bone density you achieve by the end of adolescence determines how strong your bones will be when you get older. If your bone density is not very high, you will be at much greater risk of osteoporosis when you are older. Osteoporosis can be a very serious problem, leading to fractures, pain and disability, so it is not to be taken lightly.

So how thin is too thin?

This is one question a lot of people want answered. The simple fact is, though, it is not that simple. Some people will start to experience problems because of their weight loss, or restricted diet, before others. So for one person simply going on a very strict diet can trigger changes such as loss of periods (for women), dizzy spells or problems with anaemia. For others their health seems to be more weight dependent, and it is only once weight falls below a certain point that problems are encountered. However, there are some fairly reliable rules you can apply, based on your weight and height, to calculate your risk of having some of the problems I have talked about. But bear in mind that things do not always work like this and some people may have trouble much sooner.

You have probably heard of the body mass index (BMI). This is a measure that gives you an idea of whether your weight is OK for your height. So someone who is very tall will generally weigh more than someone who is very short. To calculate BMI you divide your weight in kilograms by your height in metres squared:

$$BMI = \frac{weight\ (kg)}{height\ (m)^2}$$

A healthy BMI is generally agreed to be between 20 and 25. Once you fall outside this range you need to be more careful. It is important to realize that your height does make a difference. So if you are 5 ft 3 in, your healthy weight would fall between just over 8 stone and just over 10 stone. However, if you are taller – say, 5 ft 8 in – you should weigh roughly between 9½ stone and nearly 20 stone. BMI is not always a good measure of healthy weight because it assumes an average build. So, for example, if you are very lean and muscular you will weigh more (muscle weighs more than fat) and therefore have a higher BMI. This kind of flaw in the system has been well publicized recently, but BMI does give us an objective idea of whether our weight is likely to be healthy or not.

So, what if you are underweight? Well, the research suggests that there are certain critical levels. A BMI below 19 or 20 is certainly considered underweight, and if your BMI is below 17 or so, then you are considered to have anorexia nervosa (unless there is another good reason for your weight to be so low). This is the level at which there is a risk of periods stopping (though this can happen much earlier in some people), and at which the body has to start using alternative stores of fuel. If weight continues to fall, then obviously things get more serious. Once BMI falls below around 15, there is a real risk of organ problems and physical symptoms. It is extremely important that medical advice is sought. Anyone with a BMI of 12 or lower needs to get medical attention within twenty-four hours – it is that serious.

The risks of obesity

People generally know more about the impact that being overweight has on the body, so I am not going to go into too much detail. But, for those people whose eating disorder leads them to gain weight, putting on an excessive amount can leave them at risk of many health problems later on in life. In BMI terms, anything from 25 to 30 is considered overweight, and over 30 is obese. Obesity is linked with many chronic health problems, including heart disorders, stroke, diabetes and arthritis. It is also linked to various cancers, and an increased risk of infertility and problems in pregnancy.

Finally, one thing that surprises many people is that often those who are obese are also struggling with the impact of various deficiencies. If your diet is controlled by an eating disorder, you run the risk of it being rather unbalanced and therefore, in spite of your weight being high, your body can actually show some of the signs of malnutrition.

Do not delay seeking help

If this chapter has led you to have *any* concerns about your health, particularly ones related to the serious risks that starvation and restricting your diet can have, it is important that you go to see your GP *as soon as possible* (that is, today or tomorrow, not in a few weeks).

If you are trying to think about where you want to go (or don't want to end up) with your eating disorder, the last thing you want is for a health emergency to take your choices away from you. Too many people who think it will never happen to them find themselves forced to go into hospital because their health (and weight) has become critical. So make sure your GP is keeping an eye on your health, and take the opportunity to discuss some of these issues with him or her.

For more on going to your GP, including how to do it if it seems like the most terrifying idea, see Chapter 11.

3 The problem with purging

This is a very important chapter if you, like many people, are currently caught in a cycle that involves some method of purging food you have eaten in an attempt to avoid putting on weight. And this does not involve only those with eating disorders. Research shows that some purging behaviours are quite common among those who are trying to control their weight.

The simple truth is that purging does not work. By this I mean it does not stop you gaining weight, it does not help you regain control over your eating and it does not make you feel better about what you have eaten. I realize this might be difficult to take in – scary even. But bear with me as I explain what I mean.

Perhaps the worst thing about purging is the impact it has on the control (or lack of it) you have over your eating. People typically learn or develop a purging behaviour, so the day after they feel they have overeaten, seized with panic and worry about putting on weight, they try something they hope will stop that from happening. Some people try lots of methods until they find one that works. Some use more than one method. Whatever they settle on, they believe it stops them from putting on weight because of what they have eaten.

This is actually very dangerous because the next time they lose control and overeat, or are tempted to do so – the moment they swallow that food – is no longer the 'point of no return' because now they believe there is something they can do to stop the food from being absorbed. What this means is that binges tend to develop – and worsen over time. The longer someone goes on controlling and trying to restrict their eating, the more likely they are to start having binge episodes, and adding a purging phase makes that even worse.

So purging doesn't help you control your eating at all. Neither does it make you feel any better. In fact it makes your eating worse, and intensifies the feelings you are struggling with. Instinctively most people know that, but the lure of a possible solution – a way to get rid of the panic and anxiety that eating has brought – is too great.

The other reason purging does not work is that it does not do what you think it does. For example, let's look at laxative abuse. This is an increasingly common form of purging, when people take the type of laxative that irritates the bowel, causing it to start contracting more and more and speeding things along. The idea is that because the food does not stay in there as long, it won't be absorbed. Most people who do this, though, will admit that they are really after two things: the feeling of emptiness they get when the laxatives have taken effect, and the weight loss – that is, the change in the numbers on the scales when they weigh themselves. So if you have had a bad weekend and feel you have overeaten, you think that taking laxatives will leave you feeling empty and more in control, *and* will mean that you lose weight.

Sadly, it is not that straightforward. Food absorption is a complicated process, with different things happening at different stages. Laxatives take their effect quite far down the bowel, and the way they work is by moving the waste more quickly along the part of the bowel where usually water is reabsorbed into the body. As a result, the waste stays more fluid and therefore passes out more quickly and easily.

So, when it feels as if things are moving through more

quickly, this is correct to some degree. The passage of waste through that last bit of the bowel is usually quite slow in order for as much water as possible to be conserved. So speeding it up can make a difference. But the absorption of nutrients and calorific matter happens much further up the bowel and therefore is not really affected. What you do lose plenty of is water. Water is heavy, and a large proportion of the human body is water. So yes, if you weigh yourself before and after the laxatives have had their effect, you will see a weight loss. However, this will be because of the water you have lost and not a real weight loss. As soon as you rehydrate, you will see that weight go back up. Of course, lots of people then think they have put weight on and that can start the panic cycle off again. In fact, because taking lots of laxatives can cause such swings in water balance, weight can go up and down quite a lot, which certainly adds to the feeling of being out of control.

The really important thing about the effect of laxatives, though, is that not only water is lost. Dissolved in that water are lots of vital chemicals called electrolytes, and the levels of these in the body are absolutely crucial because they control electrical impulses, including the way the heart beats. So if you lose too many of these electrolytes you risk developing a deficiency. The most common one is hypo-(meaning too low) kalaemia, which is when the level of potassium falls too low. If this happens, you can go into heart failure and risk developing fits. So it isn't just that laxatives don't have the effect people think – it is also that they have an extremely negative effect you may not know about.

As well as this serious risk, taking laxatives over a long period of time can really mess up the way the bowel works. Waste is moved along the bowel by each muscle along it contracting in turn – a bit like the way a worm moves. If these muscles are irritated (which is what these laxatives generally do), they start to contract faster and all out of synch. This might be experienced as stomach cramps and an urgent need to get to the toilet – very similar to the way you feel if you get 'holiday tummy' or something similar. If this carries on, then the bowel can become badly affected, and people develop either constipation or persistent diarrhoea, or a mixture of both. There are even more serious problems when the bowel basically stops working completely and waste just builds up. So it really isn't worth the risk.

Another common purging technique is to make yourself sick. This has become more common as it has been more widely talked about, and exactly how people do it varies, but some people get so used to doing it that they find it very easy. Once again, however, it simply isn't as effective as you would think. Studies indicate that the reason most people do not gain weight is because in reality they don't eat as much as they think they do, not because of the effect of the vomiting. They restrict themselves so much between binges that on the whole they are just not overeating as badly as they fear. It is rare for someone to be very effective in making themselves sick. Anyone who has ever seen a child throw up will be able to tell you that they seem to produce an enormous volume, and often it looks as if the stomach must be empty when actually it is not. A similar phenomenon means that self-induced vomiting is much less effective than you would think.

Again the problem with self-induced vomiting is that a lot of water is lost, and with it valuable electrolytes. So again you might see an apparent weight loss because of this water loss, but it is not what it seems. And as with abusing laxatives, the more often you do it, and especially if you also restrict your eating, the more you are at risk of suffering serious consequences from the loss of these chemicals.

There are, of course, other minor risks too. The acid in vomit eats away at teeth, and dental problems can be the first clue that someone is struggling with bulimia. It also gives you very bad breath – as you might imagine. If you make yourself sick regularly, you can weaken the muscle that holds your stomach closed at the top, meaning that the acid leaks up the oesophagus (food pipe) and causes a lot of pain and discomfort. There is also a risk of damaging some of the delicate blood vessels that line the oesophagus, which leads to vomiting blood – never very pleasant. It is even possible to rupture the oesophagus completely, and this is a medical emergency. So once again, this is not by any means a risk-free method of purging.

If you do regularly purge food you have eaten, and having read this would like to stop, then I know it is a difficult and scary step. To many people it is easier to face the frightening risk of serious and long-term physical damage than to risk putting on weight. Make sure you read Chapter 8, which explains why stopping purging will probably make you feel really anxious. But be comforted by the fact that the reason you have not put on weight so far is not because of the purging. It might seem like it to you – and you might find it very hard to believe otherwise – but trust me, it is not. So, by stopping, all you are doing is giving your body a chance not to be damaged, and for the balance of water and so on to settle down.

Do not stop without help and support though. Particularly if you have been abusing laxatives, it is best to involve your GP. They might want to step you down gradually to reduce the risk of side-effects – or at least to monitor things. And it is likely you will need some help to settle your eating habits too – remember this is all a vicious cycle you have become caught up in. But do take some time to consider whether you really want to carry on with what you are doing.

An important note

If you are making yourself sick regularly (that is, more than once a day) and/or abusing laxatives, it is important that you seek medical help to check that you are not in any serious danger due to loss of electrolytes. Please see your GP *as soon as possible*. This is particularly important if your weight (BMI) is also low, or if you are not eating well. It is possible for someone to think they are OK when actually they are really ill and at risk of collapsing. Please don't think it wouldn't happen to you – it really could. Get it checked out!

4   What causes eating disorders?

Walking the path to recovery from eating disorders is certainly not easy, and there are many different challenges along the way – many things that need to be overcome or achieved. But whatever your stage on the path to recovery, there is one thing that the vast majority of people will need to have developed before they reach their destination, and that is an understanding of why they developed the eating disorder in the first place.

Now, this is often neglected. 'Let's not dwell on the past,' people proclaim. 'Let's focus on where we're going, not where we've been.' But if you do not know the real reason why you ended up with your eating disorder, you run the risk of either blaming yourself ('It's *my* fault. I was stupid enough to end up here') or of struggling with relapse if you face the same things again later on in recovery.

We all carry around a life story in our heads – a plan for what our lives will be like, who we will be, what we will do and when. Having to take time out to fight against an eating disorder is very rarely part of the plan. But it is so important that once it *does* form part of your life story you are able to understand how it fits in with everything else that makes up your life.

Eating disorders are very complicated. There is no way that one chapter like this could explain the reasons behind everyone's illness. However, there are some experiences that many sufferers have in common, and there are methods of reacting to emotions which most share. The main thing to remember is that most people with eating disorders are perfectly normal. It is simply that the hand life has dealt them, combined with the way they have learned to deal with the emotions that are thrown up, has led them to develop a problem. Eating disorders, like many other addictions, often seem at first to be a solution to a problem. They provide a promise that things will improve (once the weight is lost) and give life a focus. They offer the illusion of something that is achievable – something to aim at.

However, they are not long-term solutions at all, and in the long run they cause many more problems than they solve. Emotions build up and start to become overwhelming, and as the disorder starts to exert more and more of an influence on day-to-day life, this is affected too.

Finding a scapegoat

At the heart of any eating disorder is a basic belief that life would be better if only you were thinner. It is easy to understand how people slip into believing this – the world around us constantly equates slimness with success, achievement and happiness. Join that diet club and lose the weight, and you too could be leaping around with joy. So many people fall into the trap of believing that lie. Studies tend to find that around a quarter of women and at least half of teenage girls think that losing weight would make their lives better. But for those who develop eating disorders, this belief gets tangled up with the way they deal with negative emotions such as anxiety.

Emotions are very powerful things, and there is a whole field of research in psychology, neuroscience and psychiatry looking at what exactly they do, and what happens when there are problems with them. Not all emotions are pleasant to experience and some in particular can be very difficult. Emotions can also vary in their intensity, and when those unpleasant emotions become very intense, we all have to find strategies to help us cope.

Research suggests that a lot of people who have eating disorders struggle to cope with negative emotions – especially those related to anxiety and stress. Because they have no effective way of dealing with them, they build up a defence and try to ignore them. Instead, they focus on how bad they feel – on the physical symptoms of the emotion, and the way it makes them feel psychologically. So they will suddenly feel washed out, lethargic, fidgety and bad, but will not know why, because they have not identified that what they are experiencing is an emotion. This experience is horrible, so understandably they look for some way to avoid ever feeling that bad again – something they can change to protect themselves. But because they have not identified the real cause of how they are feeling, they look in the wrong place for something they can do to make things better.

It is then that they fall upon the scapegoat of blaming their body and weight for how they feel and for how bad their life is. When your self-esteem is low anyway, and you are not sure that you like yourself (and most eating disorders have their root in adolescence, when we are just starting to put together an idea of who we really are), the idea that improving yourself would help you to feel better is very enticing. So you blame yourself and your weight, and the emotions that started the process off are then turned inwards.

Lots of people end up feeling a very violent hatred towards themselves or parts of their body. All that anger, frustration and rage spills over and is targeted at yourself. 'I must be better,' you think, or more accurately, 'I must be thinner.' It feels as though you are the fattest person you know, and every fleshy fold is hated because to you it is evidence of how bad and wrong you are. All of the things that are wrong in your life become focused on those bits of your body, and the desire to change things grows. This is what fuels that urge to lose weight: it is the need to make positive changes, to protect yourself. People with eating disorders are often very determined, and that is directed towards what they think will provide the solution to their problems and make them better (happier) people.

The trouble with this system is that it is so effective at distracting you from the real cause of those horrid feelings that you become oblivious to the emotion behind everything. It is as if it forms a smoke screen over the original emotion that is actually causing the problem (see Figure 1). Dealing with that emotion – usually anxiety, stress or worry – becomes about changing yourself and losing weight. Instead of feeling moments when you are overwhelmed with that emotion, you will probably experience 'fat' moments, when you feel overwhelmed with a feeling of how fat you are, combined with those negative

Figure 1: The formation of emotional smoke screens

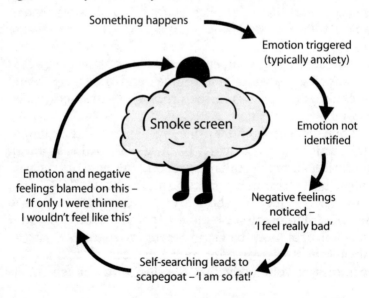

feelings. These moments often trigger binge–purge cycles, or strengthen the urge to restrict your diet.

They can also lead people to become more and more isolated because they are unable to explain how they are feeling to another person, especially if those around them just tell them they are not fat. How they feel about their body and weight has become totally detached from a reality of how they look and has become a scapegoat for the negative emotions that often overwhelm them. So, no matter how much they are told they don't look fat, or don't need to lose weight, in those moments when the emotions are overwhelming and that 'fat' feeling descends, rational arguments cease to matter, and the urge to lose weight and therefore to stop that awful feeling is overpowering.

The real cause at the root of most eating disorders will be something that triggers these kinds of powerful emotions in the first place. It is no surprise, therefore, that the kinds of experience that have been linked with an increased risk of developing an eating disorder are those things that trigger these difficult emotions: trauma, abuse, difficult family or life experiences, grief, poor self-esteem, etc. Dieting is often at the start of an eating disorder, because it is a symptom of that person's belief that success in a diet would help them to get rid of these horrible feelings. Abuse, bullying and anything that challenges your self-esteem are also very common experiences linked with eating disorders, because when you are not sure if you are a good, nice, likeable person, you are at risk of thinking in certain ways that can trigger these negative emotions (see Chapter 6).

The role of genetics
One factor that needs to be mentioned is the role genetics plays in the development of eating disorders. Over recent years, research into the genetic background to eating

disorders, especially anorexia, has grown in popularity, triggering newspaper headlines like 'Can you inherit your anorexia?'.[2]

The reality is that some genetic traits seem to make people more at risk of developing eating disorders. However, it is not as simple as one gene, or even a group of genes, 'causing' an eating disorder. Rather, it is having a certain genetic make-up that means you might be 'fertile soil' for an eating disorder: if the right conditions are present, then you might be at greater risk of developing a problem.

Some studies identify genes that might contribute to some of the practical abilities required to develop an eating disorder, such as the ability to tolerate starvation or easily make yourself sick. Others are linked to the personality factors that different sufferers display. What all of this means is that some people – and some families – might be at greater risk of eating disorders than others because they have the genetic make-up required to be able to develop one. This does not mean they are doomed to struggle with eating disorders all their lives; nor does it mean they are deficient, weak or damaged in some way. Most important of all, it does not mean that you passed on an eating disorder to your child, or that a child of yours will inevitably suffer with the same eating disorder that you did.

Hope for the future
Finally, a word on what these causes mean for your future if you are currently struggling with an eating disorder. In the vast majority of cases, it is possible for sufferers to recover from their eating disorder. This is not easy, and many people struggle with recovery, but it definitely is possible. None of the causes at the root of eating disorders

[2] *Daily Mail*, 10 April 2001

mean that you cannot recover, or that you have to become a totally different person in order to be free. You do not have to suppress your real self in order to live a life without an eating disorder. Studies looking at personality features like perfectionism, which are often a strong part of eating-disordered thoughts and behaviours, find that in recovery these personality traits persist, but the way in which they affect people has changed (see Chapter 7).

So recovery is about finding new and more positive strategies to cope with emotions, improving your self-esteem and conquering your fears, not changing who you are inside.

5 'I'm not sure I want to stop'

So far in this book we have looked at a lot of the background to eating disorders: what they are, what causes them and what effects they have. But this is a book about recovery and how to get on that path. So we will now move on to think about what is involved in recovery. For many people, deciding that they want to work on recovery is actually the hardest step in their fight against an eating disorder. They may feel very anxious about leaving it behind, find it difficult to accept letting go of goals they had set themselves, fear losing control and being forced to eat and gain weight, or worry about what recovery will really mean for them.

This chapter aims to help you make sense of those kinds of mixed feelings. Moving on from an eating disorder is a big step, and as with any difficult decision it is important to think it through clearly. It is also really important that you think long term. An eating disorder makes you think very short term – to the next meal, the next lot of exercise, the next pound lost. It is a bit like walking a long journey just looking at your feet to see where the next step will be. Many people with eating disorders stumble on like this until suddenly they find themselves somewhere they never wanted to be. Maybe the eating disorder had a huge impact on their life and meant they had to change plans such as going to university or succeeding in a career. Maybe their health became critical and they were forced to go into hospital. Whatever the outcome, they did not see it coming, because the eating disorder kept them thinking short term. So it is very important to think about what you want, not just for now, but for the future too.

Leaving behind an eating disorder is hard. You may feel that there is nothing wrong, and just wish that people would leave you alone and stop fussing. Whatever decisions you make, be very careful that you are headed somewhere you want to go. There is nothing worse than realizing that the destination of your trip was somewhere horrid only when you get there. This chapter is about helping you to think about where you are really going.

The following exercise isn't designed to try to get you to do something you wouldn't want to do, or even to make any specific decisions. It is to help you think things through clearly, taking everything into account and not missing anything important.

First of all, find a couple of big pieces of paper. I often use flipchart paper. Remember, if it turns out the paper was too big you can always fold it over or tear a bit off, but if you end up wishing you had more space, that is a lot more tricky. You will probably also find it helps to have some coloured pens. Somehow this kind of exercise is always easier if you can write in lots of different colours.

Take your first sheet of paper and draw a table with two columns. At the top of one write 'Pros' and at the top of the next write 'Cons'. The idea is to think realistically about what you get from your eating disorder, both good and bad. Some things may be physical, and some may be psychological (for example, 'It helps me to feel in control', or 'When I lose weight I feel better about myself'). You will probably find it easier to think of things for one column than for the other. Try to come up with as many things as you can for each. You might want to keep the list to hand for a few days so that when you think of new things to add, you can put them on before you forget. You might also want to ask a good friend to have a look and see if there are any things you left off the list.

Once you have done this, get your second piece of paper and draw the same two columns on it: Pros and Cons. This time, sit and have a think about where you would like to be at some stage in the future. Maybe something significant is about to happen – you're off to college, or getting married, or doing GCSEs. Or you could just look a few years into the future. What will your life be like at this point in the future if you still have the eating disorder? Once again, write down any pros and cons you can think of.

Try not to be biased or to lie when you do this – it is for you and no one else. Forget for a moment that people are nagging you or that other people have opinions. This is about you and what you think. After all, it is you who will live your life, not anyone else. In the future, the effects of your eating disorder will be experienced by you, and you alone, so try to think of all you can to fill both charts.

To help you out, here is an example chart from a girl we will call Jenny (see opposite). She was struggling with anorexia, and finding it really hard to think about leaving it behind.

How did you find this task? Were you surprised by some of the things you thought of to put in the charts? In your first chart you, like Jenny, may have had a fairly equal number of pros and cons. Or you may have had mainly pros. Or perhaps any cons you did have were things other people thought and said but you were not sure about.

All this should help you (and maybe even those around you) to understand why the eating disorder developed. An eating disorder seems all bad from the outside, but the truth is that it does have some positives at first – that's why people start to take that route in the first place. But the chances are that in the second list you had more cons than pros. That is because eating disorders are really only a short-term solution. That stage where they are mostly positive can be very short lived. Eating disorders bring with

Now (sixteen years old)

Pros	Cons
Feel more confident.	Feel tired all the time.
Helps me feel in control.	Am always cold.
People notice me.	Periods have stopped and I am scared of ending up unable to have children.
Means I cannot go to school.	Parents are always on at me.
People expect less of me.	Struggle with depression – feel really awful sometimes.
Feel better about myself when I have lost weight.	Cannot go out with friends.
People look up to me because of my self control.	

In two years' time (after A-levels)

Pros	Cons
Will still be thin.	Health will probably be really bad. Will still have no periods and might want to have kids before long.
Will still feel in control.	Will be on my own – all my friends will have gone off to university or got jobs, but I won't be able to.
People will still expect less of me.	Will be stuck with parents, as they probably won't let me get a flat while I am still ill.
	Will still be having times of feeling really terrible.
	Will I be able to cope with these? Not sure it is worth it.
	I will have missed out on going to uni, I won't be able to do the job I want to. Not sure what my life would be about.
	Would like to get married really, but this is unlikely while am still ill and stuck inside the house.
	Don't want to be known as 'the anorexic one'.
	Will probably have lost touch with old friends because they might get fed up with me being so miserable.

them so many negatives that they typically end up causing many more problems than they solve. So whereas it is important to accept and understand that you have got some positive things from your eating disorder, at the same time it is really vital that you think about the negatives, which are likely to grow in number the longer you carry on.

Remember that this task is not designed to push you into making a decision. It is there to help you think things through thoroughly and to help you make sure you are not overlooking something important. If you can, show the charts to someone you feel able to chat to and who will help you to look at the results. Talk about how this changes your thinking about the eating disorders (if at all). Talk about the things you learned from doing this task. If you come to any definite conclusions, write them down.

Ultimately, if the second chart revealed that things might get much harder in the future, this implies that the course you are on at the moment needs to change at some point between now and then so that you will not end up in that place. Think about the destination of the path you are on. Do you want to go there? Making a decision to change that course at some stage is the first step towards recovery (see Chapter 10 for more on recovery).

Part 2

Problems and potential pitfalls

Issues commonly associated with eating disorders

6 Unhelpful thinking styles

Low self-esteem is something we hear a lot about these days. Whether it is on a TV chat show, part of a politician's speech or something mentioned in a book or report, low self-esteem is proposed as being at the root of many mental health problems – as well as many other difficulties we face in our society. What isn't explained as often is why low self-esteem has such a big impact on people. The answer is that very often it is because of the way it affects their thinking.

You may be surprised by the suggestion that something as simple as how you think could have such a big impact on you. Surely it is things that happen to us in our life, or perhaps things to do with our biology and genetics, that leave us prone to struggling with things like depression. The reality is that yes, these things do play a role, but how much these things affect us has a lot to do with the way they affect our thinking. Research shows us that certain patterns of thinking are strongly linked with negative emotions, anxiety and depression. So if something traumatic happens to you, it will affect you much more if it pushes you into these cycles of negative thinking. Similarly, a personality feature such as perfectionism is much more likely to have a negative impact on you if it becomes something that triggers these kinds of thoughts (more about this in the next chapter).

Patterns of thinking
These patterns of thinking are so powerful that a treatment based on getting rid of them is now the treatment of choice

for many mental health problems. This is called cognitive behaviour therapy (CBT), and it is a part of most treatment programmes for eating disorders. CBT involves identifying and understanding the way in which certain styles of thinking affect someone, and then helping them to challenge the beliefs that underlie those thoughts.

There are basically four styles of thinking that are part of this group. I like to call them 'unhelpful' thinking styles. It isn't that any one of them is particularly awful, and in fact thinking in some of these ways is terribly common and probably part of everyday life for most of us. But if you get caught up in thinking in these ways, then you will find that it magnifies negative emotions, extends dark moods and generally makes you feel fairly rotten.

UNHELPFUL THINKING STYLE 1: BEING TOO NEGATIVE
This is really someone who is the typical pessimist and tends to pick out anything negative they can find in what happens. It breaks down into two categories: looking back and recalling the negative things, and looking forward and predicting negative things. So someone who is prone to this type of thinking will look back through their day and only remember the negative things that happened. They will recall the conversation that went wrong, the thing they forgot to do and the friend they forgot to phone, and focus on those things when thinking about their day. Or they will think about tomorrow, or next week, and only expect negative things.

This style of thinking is one we can easily slip into when we are already feeling sad or depressed for some reason, because our brains find it easier to recall memories that match our current mood. So if you are feeling sad and lonely, you might find that the memories that pop into your mind are times when you felt the same way. The trouble with thinking like this is that it makes you believe your life is built up only of negative things. Typically people miss so many positive things that have happened, or are likely to happen, because they are focusing so hard on those negatives. This is the classic pessimist, whose glass is always half empty and who believes that anything that can go wrong probably will.

UNHELPFUL THINKING STYLE 2: BLACK AND WHITE THINKING
This is a thinking style that some people in particular find themselves prone to. People who think in this way categorize the world very clearly into two possibilities: right or wrong, success or failure, good or bad, acceptable or forbidden. They do not accept that there is any grey in between these extremes. So, a practical example of this might be if you were taking a test or exam, to have in mind a score that represents being 'successful' to you. Someone who is prone to black and white thinking will see any score less than that mark as a total failure – even if they missed it by only a couple of marks. They are also unlikely to make any allowances, say if they were unwell on that day, or if there was another reason they did not perform to their usual standard.

It is a style of thinking that leads people who suffer from eating disorders to form clear categories in their mind as to which foods are 'good' and which are 'bad'; which they can/should eat and which are 'unacceptable'. Almost everyone who has suffered from an eating disorder could tell you which foods went on which list in their mind.

The trouble with thinking in this way is that the world is very rarely that clear cut. It leaves you prone to feeling you have failed, and to trying to exert too much control over your life, which can lead you into trouble. If you often think in this way, you are probably also prone to being this black and white over the way you feel about your life. So if you look back over your day and can find anything negative about it, you may well feel that your day was a total disaster. This kind of 'all or nothing' thinking means that you will probably have very few 'good' days, because having a day that is 100 per cent good is very unusual.

UNHELPFUL THINKING STYLE 3: CATASTROPHIZING
This is a rather nasty name for a style of thinking that I believe most of us slip into from time to time. It describes the way you feel when your thinking is influenced by stress, tiredness or anxiety – and as a result you make great jumps in logic from one negative thing that has happened in the past to other negative things that you feel are almost guaranteed to happen in the future. So you make a silly comment in a class, lecture or work meeting, say, and when you get to thinking about it, your next thought is to panic that your friends will think you are stupid, no one will ever respect you again, you will probably never do well in your career, and your life will be a total disaster. It is difficult to write this down without it looking slightly silly, but we have all had moments when we feel this way and it really doesn't feel funny at the time. It feels as if we have said the wrong thing, and now our life will be a total disaster as a result.

People are often prone to thinking in this way if they are struggling in general with anxiety or stress, and of course it makes them feel even more stressed and anxious as a result. There is a sense of losing control in the way the thoughts jump forward in time and that is what fuels the panic. If you get caught up in thinking in this way, then the chances are you will end up experiencing extremes of emotion and find it very difficult to get rid of those feelings.

UNHELPFUL THINKING STYLE 4: NEGATIVE MIND-READING
Would you describe yourself as someone who is good at

'reading people'? Do you feel that you are good at knowing what people are thinking? Well, if you do, be careful, because people who feel like this are often at risk of slipping into this last unhelpful way of thinking. Negative mind-reading is all about feeling that you are good at knowing what other people are thinking, but if you look at the thoughts that people who are prone to this 'see' in those around them, they nearly always pick up on negative thoughts. So they worry about people thinking bad things about them, or being upset because of things they have said. They can become paranoid, worrying that people are laughing at them or talking about them. Very rarely, if ever, do they ascribe a positive thought to someone, such as, 'They are looking at me because they think I look good.' Much more common are thoughts that make them feel bad, ashamed, guilty or embarrassed.

The problem with this style of thinking, apart from the negative emotions it causes, is that it can lead people to become very isolated and to withdraw into themselves, which then leaves them plenty of time to dwell on things and no doubt slip into the other three thinking patterns listed above.

Being aware of your thinking

Did you recognize any of these unhelpful thinking styles in yourself? As I have said, we are all prone to some of them some of the time, but if you struggle with times where you feel particularly low, or would describe yourself as feeling bad and not knowing why, it may well be that these thinking styles are triggering, prolonging or worsening your bad mood. It is certainly worth being aware of them, because if you can become aware of when you are thinking in this way, it can immediately help you to feel less out of control.

Times when these thinking styles dominate are also commonly linked to eating disorder behaviour. This happens for one of two reasons. The first is that sometimes you feel really terrible but do not know why. When this happens, naturally you want to try to find something you can change that will protect you from feeling as bad as you do ever again (see Chapter 4 for more on this). Because you do not know what caused those feelings, often the only thing you can change is something about yourself. This is where the belief that life would be better if you were thinner can kick in. If the only cause you can find for feeling so bad is within yourself, then all those negative emotions can turn inwards and that self-hatred can be very strong. It is then all too easy to blame yourself, and to feel that if you just change yourself for the better, you will not feel so bad. So, often this triggers those 'feeling fat' moments, or can make you feel really terrible about yourself. Sometimes it turns you inwards so that you analyse every tiny thing about yourself, looking for something that could be wrong and could be causing the way you feel. Again, when the ideals presented to us are all so much thinner than is going to be normal for most of us, it is easy to slip into a pattern of thinking that if only we were thinner, we would feel better.

The second reason these thinking styles are linked to eating disorders is because of the way certain behaviours, such as eating, can be linked to our emotions. Nearly half of people surveyed admit that they eat to change their mood, and it is well recognized that some people eat in response to feeling low or depressed or anxious. So eating can in some way be an attempt to cope with negative emotions and can therefore be triggered by these thought patterns. Particularly in those who struggle with binge-eating, binges can often be strongly linked to times when these thinking styles trigger really low moods.

Using CBT

So how do you find out if thinking in one of these ways is making you feel bad? Well, that is basically what CBT helps you to do, and then it moves on to challenge whether the assumptions you have made about yourself are right or not. If you are receiving treatment for an eating disorder, then the chances are that CBT will be a part of this. If not, then you may be able to find a private counsellor who can work through this kind of approach with you. If in doubt, talk it over with your GP.

You may be reading this chapter having already had an experience of treatment using CBT that was not very positive. Some people find it very frustrating because it does not look into the background of *why* you think in the way you do. It simply moves forwards and works to change the unhelpful patterns of thinking. CBT is not a substitute for understanding the background to why an eating disorder developed, and ideally should be used in conjunction with other approaches. However, it can be a really useful tool in helping someone to feel more in control of their emotions, and to decrease the intensity of negative emotions which may be strongly linked to some of the thoughts and behaviours involved with the eating disorder. Try to give it a fair go. CBT is not blaming you for everything you are suffering. However, it is saying that you can change some of how you feel by taking charge of your thoughts again and challenging some of the things you believe. In a way, working through CBT is like being your own detective, analysing how some of the thought patterns you have slipped into are triggering your emotional difficulties. The early stages may seem fairly cold and even boring. You are likely to be asked to keep a diary of your thinking, which may be difficult, particularly if you are feeling very distressed. Do persist with this, because the insight you are likely to gain can be really valuable. If you can get to a stage where you recognize and challenge these thought patterns, you will find that your emotions become much more stable, and this will probably help you to work on the other things involved in your eating disorder.

7 Perfectly flawed or perfectly driven: when is perfectionism a bad thing?

Of all the personality factors often linked with eating disorders, and anorexia in particular, the most commonly written about in media articles and books is that of perfectionism. But what is perfectionism, and is it always a bad thing? And is it really so closely linked to eating disorders?

Being a perfectionist

Someone who is very perfectionistic places a high value on getting things absolutely right. They tend to set very high standards and will push themselves hard in order to achieve them. They find it difficult to accept any kind of failure or to reduce these goals, and may ignore negative consequences as they push towards achievements. Perfectionism often extends to all areas of a person's life, and they may only take part in activities and pursuits in which they can excel.

Perfectionism as a personality trait is indeed strongly linked with eating disorders, and especially anorexia nervosa. Scoring highly on measures of perfectionism is a risk factor for anorexia (meaning that you are at greater risk of developing it if you score highly), and the genetic trait towards perfectionism seems to be one of those inherited dispositions that may influence the risk of anorexia.

One of the important things to know about perfectionism,

though, is that although it can be strongly linked with an eating disorder, it does not disappear once people have recovered. Someone who has recovered from anorexia is still more likely to score higher on scales of perfectionism than someone who has never suffered. Therefore, although perfectionism is linked with some eating disorders, perfectionism itself is not all bad.

When is perfectionism good?

If you are someone who has a tendency towards perfectionism, you probably know it. Reading the description above, you may have recognized yourself in that, or maybe there are elements very familiar to you. However, being perfectionistic in itself is not automatically a bad thing. Sometimes perfectionism can be a very strong attribute of someone's character. It is this kind of personality trait that drives people on to achieve great things, and many of the world's great achievers are probably very perfectionistic people. But for some people their tendency to drive themselves that hard can start to cause problems.

When is perfectionism bad?

People who work with eating disorders and other areas of mental health tend to talk about two kinds of perfectionism: what is called 'functional' (helpful) perfectionism and something called 'clinical' perfectionism.[3] It is the clinical perfectionism that tends to be found alongside eating disorders and other mental health problems.

So-called 'clinical' perfectionism generally has one main feature that makes it problematic: the person's self-worth is largely or exclusively dependent on them achieving perfectionism in the things they do. This means that if they

[3] Shafran, R. Cooper, Z. and Fairburn, C.G., 2002, 'Clinical Perfectionism: A Cognitive-Behavioural Analysis', *Behav. Res. Ther* 40 (7) 773–79.

fail in their aim to be perfect, they feel they have no value and their life and achievements may be worthless. This kind of perfectionism is an extreme version of that which can be a drive for achievement. In place of the preference for success and motivation to succeed that comes with functional perfectionism is a morbid fear of failure. To fail is unacceptable and very frightening. The standards set can become very high and sometimes unrealistic. There are often things that can only be done with some suffering for the person – maybe they have to work until they are exhausted or until their arms ache with pain. Maybe they have to be the last one to stop work and go to bed each day – or the person who runs that little bit further or faster than all their friends. Then if a goal is achieved, instead of feeling satisfied and happy, the person often feels that this is an indicator that they had not set the goal high enough. They may undermine their achievement, or decide that the goal was too low and set a higher one. The goals gradually increase in difficulty until they become unrealistic and failure is inevitable. Then when the person cannot meet their goal, this feels like a confirmation to them that they are really useless and have no value.

Let's look at a case study. It shows how this kind of perfectionism can become tied up with an eating disorder. Figure 2 opposite shows how it can become a vicious cycle.

Case study

'Sally is eighteen and about to sit her A-level exams. She developed anorexia about six months ago, while in her first year of sixth form. As well as the anorexia, she finds herself more and more restricted in what she can do because of her tendency to be perfectionistic. New activities tend to very quickly become lists of standards she has to meet, and she finds it very hard to do anything 'just for fun'.

Figure 2: The vicious cycle of clinical perfectionism

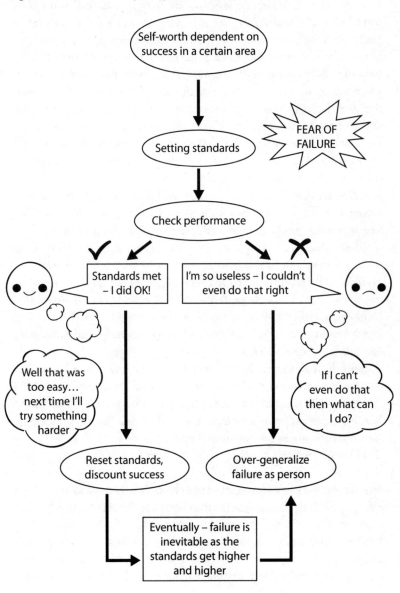

61

'She recently took up football because one of her friends already played. However, whereas at first it was fun, soon she found that if she did not practise every day she began to feel guilty and very anxious about what would happen in the next game. She therefore began to practise every day. At first this was just kicking the ball around for a while and practising some manoeuvres. Soon though she started to time herself and decided that she should practise for an hour every day. She felt she had to do this, rain or shine, and even when she was very busy with other things. Also, the way she practised started to change – as she worked out some specific exercises she began to count them, and soon was doing each twenty times. The practice session became very strict and followed a firm routine. When she did not perform as well as she wanted (for example, not scoring a goal every match), she increased her training until she was practising for two hours every day – half an hour in the morning before school and an hour and a half in the evening. The trouble was that when she did do well – scoring three goals even in one match – she felt that this was due not to her practising but to something else – for example, the keeper in one case had not been playing properly and had let her goals in. One week she had actually injured her ankle playing in a match at the weekend, but she still forced herself to go out that week and practise just as much as before, despite the pain. She complained that it was no longer fun – that it had become just another chore she had to do. Even the matches weren't fun any more because they had become such a test of whether or not she had practised enough in the week.'

So does perfectionism need to be treated?

Well, perfectionism itself does not necessarily need to be treated. However, the elements of perfectionism that can be problematic generally do need to be addressed. For people whose perfectionism is linked to an eating disorder, their eating is likely to be another area in which they have started to apply these kinds of perfectionistic, rigid rules. This means that until this kind of perfectionism is challenged, they will find it very hard to break out of this type of control.

Perfectionism can also mean that people become prone to one or more of the common unhelpful thinking styles outlined in the last chapter. Things like 'all or nothing' thinking are often more common in those who have a perfectionistic personality, and if that pattern of thinking has become linked with difficult emotions, or with things like self-harm or an eating disorder, then looking at this issue of perfectionism can help to deal with that problem.

For other people, perfectionism does not need to be treated at all. They may feel that it does not cause them any problems, or perhaps these kinds of features are not really a part of their eating disorder. In these cases there is no need to 'treat' something that is not causing a problem. Remember that perfectionism can be a very positive trait, so we need to be careful not to automatically think of it as a bad thing. The reality is that there is no such thing as a bad personality type. All types of personality have aspects that are positive – and aspects that are negative. It is too easy to look at ourselves and see only the negative, so make sure that you turn your own negative tendencies around and think about how they can also be positive. For example, if you want something done and you want it done well, someone who has a tendency to be perfectionistic is often a great person to ask. They will probably do the job reliably and to a high standard. But if you just need a job doing as quickly as possible and the standard isn't important, that same person would get tied up in fussing over details that someone else would move past.

When perfectionism has become a negative issue in someone's life, often they do want to be able to be free of some of the ways they are controlled by it. So, for example, people want to know how they can avoid a certain pastime becoming just another chore, or how they can break away from the goals in another part of their life that are starting to cause them difficulties. For others, perfectionism can start to spoil relationships with family and friends, and this becomes something they want to regain control of. In this case, challenging these more difficult aspects of perfectionism, rather than the perfectionism itself, can be effective.

How do you 'treat' perfectionism?

There are three main things that treatment might aim to help you do:

1. Treatment can aim to stop the achievement of perfection being the only thing you get any real value from. This would work therefore on finding other areas of interest and activities that make you feel good, and also work on developing your foundation feeling of value, learning who you are and were meant to be, and finding a security in that.

2. Another action point for treatment is to look at the way in which perfectionism is often used to decrease anxiety. People sometimes talk about their goals being like a list they can go down, and if they can tick off all the things on the list, they know they do not have to worry about anything. Finding other ways of decreasing anxiety and coping with stress makes the perfectionism less powerful.

3. The final way of working with perfectionism is to look at what makes functional (helpful) perfectionism different from the kind that causes problems. The aspects that belong to more clinical perfectionism can

then be challenged and worked on, so that the person is less at the mercy of their own drive for perfectionism.

So, overall, treatment aims to identify perfectionism where it is a problem and understand which aspects are the difficult ones. Your goal, if you are in treatment, should not necessarily be to a lower level of perfectionism, but rather to stop it from having such a big impact on how you feel about yourself. Try to identify the bits of your perfectionism that may be particularly unhelpful and difficult, and think about how you can reduce the costs of perfectionism to you – that is, identify where it is making your life difficult and work to challenge and reduce this difficulty. Finally, treatment should help you to find alternatives to attain self-worth and reduce anxiety, and work to increase the number of interests you have.

All of these things will hopefully help you to channel your tendency towards perfectionism into positive things and change the way it affects your life.

8 Fanning the flame: dealing with anxiety

Of all the emotions that humans are born with, anxiety perhaps has the clearest apparent function: it serves to warn us of potentially threatening situations and ensures that we take action. Anxiety is very difficult to ignore and perhaps for this reason is one of the most unpleasant emotions to experience long term. It is also the emotion that could be most often accused of causing problems. For many people anxiety becomes far too common a companion, and is triggered by all kinds of situations and experiences. In addition to this, the way we instinctively react to anxiety can also mean that it becomes more of a problem.

Making a link

To understand anxiety you have to think about the way your brain links events. Many people will have heard of the old experiment carried out by Pavlov. When Pavlov took a group of dogs and measured how much saliva they produced, he recorded, not surprisingly, that they salivated much more just before they were fed than at other times. He then started to ring a bell just before each mealtime, and at other times of the day. After a while, whenever he rang the bell the dogs still salivated more, even if there was no food present.

What Pavlov had shown was that our brains start to link stimuli with consequences, and as a result our behaviour can change. The dogs had learned that a bell meant food was probably coming soon, and their behaviour (the salivation) started to change so that they reacted not to the real stimulus (the food) but to the thing that had become associated with it (the bell). Similarly, our brains can link things that happen with the consequences to make very strong connections.

This same tendency can occur with anxiety, and one particular episode in my life will serve as an example. When I was about seven, my family were on holiday in Italy, and we got into a lift during a thunderstorm. While we were in the lift there was a power cut, and the lift stopped between floors. As a result of what was actually a very short period of time when we were stuck, I developed a fear of lifts. Understandably I was scared to go in one in case the same thing happened again. I had started to link a stimulus (the lift) with an outcome (getting stuck) and the anxiety that went with it. So what did I start to do? Quite sensibly (you would think) I began to avoid going in lifts. This, I thought, would decrease my anxiety, as I would no longer be exposed to the thing that made me anxious. But the trouble with anxiety is that the minute you start to do this, the tables turn. So once I started to avoid lifts my anxiety grew and grew. Eventually I got to the stage where I could not even stand in front of a lift without feeling very anxious, and to go in one was a major undertaking that I avoided at all costs.

Worst case scenario
So why does anxiety react like this? Anxiety is an emotion that always has a focus – something you are scared will happen. I like to call this the worst case scenario (WCS). In my case the WCS was getting stuck in a lift again. Whenever you feel anxious, always ask yourself, 'What is the WCS I am scared of?' When something makes us anxious we often start to avoid it or do something that we feel protects us from the WCS – whatever it is. So I stopped going into lifts, because that way I was not exposed to my fear of the WCS (getting stuck). The thing is, most of those WCSs are unlikely to ever actually happen. So in fact even if I had gone in lots of lifts I

probably wouldn't have got stuck again. But the important thing was that I believed the only reason it didn't happen was because of what I did – or didn't do.

Anxiety is like a fire burning in a corner: if you throw more fuel onto it, it gets bigger and bigger (see Figure 3). The minute we start to believe that our action was the only thing that stopped the WCS, we feel more in control (at first), but what we are really doing is throwing fuel onto the fire that is our anxiety. Why? Well, because the next time

Figure 3: Feeding the fire of anxiety

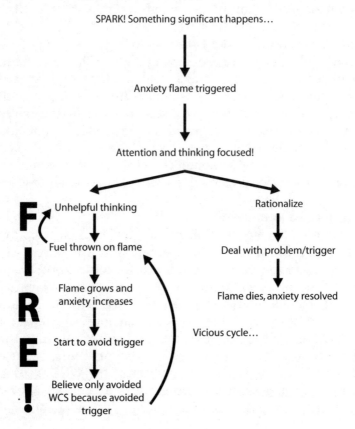

SPARK! Something significant happens…

Anxiety flame triggered

Attention and thinking focused!

Unhelpful thinking

Rationalize

F

Fuel thrown on flame

Deal with problem/trigger

I

Flame grows and anxiety increases

Flame dies, anxiety resolved

R

Start to avoid trigger

Vicious cycle…

E

Believe only avoided WCS because avoided trigger

!

we are faced with the same situation and the same WCS, we think, 'The only reason this didn't happen last time is because of what I did,' so we have to do it again.

And for a little while doing whatever it is keeps the anxiety down. But anxiety, like a fire, is very greedy and it creeps forward. So maybe you are afraid of getting burgled, and you check every night that your doors are locked. Then one week, as well as checking the doors, you check the windows – just once because you are feeling particularly anxious. But then after that you have to check the doors *and* windows every time, because what if the only reason the WCS didn't happen was because you did that extra thing? So little by little anxiety gains ground, and grows. And as we get more anxious we start to do more and more to try to keep ourselves safe, but the fear grows because we believe that if we don't do these things, that WCS will happen.

So how does this work in eating disorders? Well, for most sufferers the WCS is getting fat (or failing to lose weight). This is because they believe that the reason they are feeling so bad is because they are overweight and that losing weight would help them to be happier and feel better. In order to try to decrease the anxiety and avoid that WCS, most people plan to go on a strict diet, and/or start to exercise more and/or do something else such as taking laxatives/diet pills. With each of those examples the anxiety creeps forward, so the avoidant behaviours grow. So maybe at first you restrict your eating a little, have a short list of foods you definitely avoid and set yourself a reasonably sensible goal. But then one day you are feeling particularly anxious, so you eat a little less, or move the goal a bit, or add another food to the 'forbidden' list. Over time that list grows, and the restriction gets more and more severe.

The same happens with exercise. Maybe at first you start to go to the gym in order to try to get fit and help towards losing weight. But you want to make sure you go 'enough', so you aim at three times a week. All very good, but then one week you have some spare time, so you actually go four times. The next week the anxiety kicks in, and you feel you have to go four times. Before long you are having to fit in a trip to the gym every day and you are exhausted and letting people down as you simply don't have the time to do other things.

Similarly many people who are abusing laxatives or diet pills find it very hard to stop, even when they find out that taking these pills is not actually helping them keep their weight down. Why? Because taking these pills is actually something they do in order to keep their anxiety down – to avoid that dreaded WCS. Most people start out taking the recommended dose, but very often that greedy anxiety means that before long they are taking massive overdoses of the pills because they are so anxious and scared of putting on weight.

There is a wonderful illustration of anxiety in one of the Harry Potter stories.[4] Harry, for those of you who have not read the books or seen the films, is a boy wizard who goes to a boarding school where he learns about magic. Anyway, earlier in the book in question Harry has had a lesson learning how to fight a particular kind of monster called a Bogart, which has the ability to turn into whatever you fear most when you confront it. Harry is having a conversation with one of the teachers about what the Bogart would turn into if he faced it. He describes how for him it would turn into something called a Dementor: a horrible monster that makes you relive your worst memories and the worst moments in your life. The teacher is impressed, because what that implies is that Harry's worst fear is fear itself, and he responds, 'Very wise, Harry, very wise.' This is exactly the point: what makes anxiety problems develop is not the likelihood of the thing you are scared of – the WCS – actually happening at all, but

[4] J. K. Rowling, *Harry Potter and the Prisoner of Azkaban*, Bloomsbury Publishing plc, 2004.

your fear of it happening, and what that makes you do. The thing to be scared of is not the WCS, but the way anxiety can creep forward and gradually take over your life.

Using road diagrams

So, bearing that in mind, how do we fight anxiety? Well, the first thing to do is ask yourself, 'What is the WCS?' What is that thing that you are scared of happening if you don't do whatever it is? Then you need to be very brave and look rationally into how likely that thing is. Maybe get someone to help you here. So if you are eating very little, and someone has promised to help make sure you don't lose control, and in fact you are still losing weight to the extent that your life is at risk, the chances of you becoming fat in the blink of an eye are tiny. Similarly, although exercise is good and important for everyone, missing one bike ride or gym session this week is not going to make you fat. In my case, I had to accept that actually thousands of people use lifts every day and very few actually get stuck.

The second step is then to start to win back ground from the anxiety. One way you can begin to do this is by drawing what I call a *road diagram* (see pages 72–73 for two examples). Think about what you do at the moment because you are scared of that WCS. Maybe there are lots of things, such as the way you restrict your diet or the way you force yourself to exercise. Then get one piece of paper for each thing that you do and focus on one at a time. For example, perhaps you have to go to the gym every day and do at least thirty minutes' exercise. Then think, 'What would I like to be able to do?' Maybe you would like to be able to be flexible – sometimes go to the gym, sometimes not; maybe you would like to go a couple of times a week but have it not matter if you missed a day. In the top left-hand corner of your paper write the first thing: where you are now. In one of the bottom corners write where you would like to get to.

Figure 4: Road diagram for someone trying to stop abusing laxatives

Take laxatives every day. Always take more than the recommended dose. Particularly take them after a binge

START

See Dr and admit I am abusing laxatives. Get health checked out – in case they have made me ill. Get his support in stopping taking them. Take this chart in (completed!) to show him

Reduce the number I take so that I only take the recommended dose each day. Ask a friend to keep a copy of the chart so someone is making sure I keep working through it

Get a pot and put in it each week the money I would have spent on extra on laxatives. Use it to treat myself (non food treats!)

Take one day each week where I don't take the laxatives

Take two days each week where I don't take them

On the days when I take them reduce the dose I take to half the amount

Reduce how often I take them to every other day

Stop using them after a binge. Write a reminder card about how they do not stop you absorbing food to remind me why not to take them

Reduce taking them to every two days

Reduce taking them to twice a week

Reduce taking them to once a week

Reduce taking them to once a month

FINISH!!

Have ceremonial burning of laxative packet to mark that I am never going to take them again. Buy something nice to treat myself and mark my achievement

Figure 5: Road diagram for someone trying to improve the variety in their diet

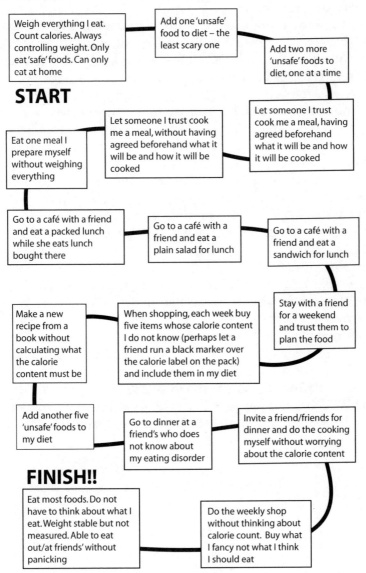

Weigh everything I eat. Count calories. Always controlling weight. Only eat 'safe' foods. Can only eat at home

START

Add one 'unsafe' food to diet – the least scary one

Add two more 'unsafe' foods to diet, one at a time

Let someone I trust cook me a meal, without having agreed beforehand what it will be and how it will be cooked

Let someone I trust cook me a meal, having agreed beforehand what it will be and how it will be cooked

Eat one meal I prepare myself without weighing everything

Go to a café with a friend and eat a packed lunch while she eats lunch bought there

Go to a café with a friend and eat a plain salad for lunch

Go to a café with a friend and eat a sandwich for lunch

Make a new recipe from a book without calculating what the calorie content must be

When shopping, each week buy five items whose calorie content I do not know (perhaps let a friend run a black marker over the calorie label on the pack) and include them in my diet

Stay with a friend for a weekend and trust them to plan the food

Add another five 'unsafe' foods to my diet

Go to dinner at a friend's who does not know about my eating disorder

Invite a friend/friends for dinner and do the cooking myself without worrying about the calorie content

FINISH!!

Eat most foods. Do not have to think about what I eat. Weight stable but not measured. Able to eat out/at friends' without panicking

Do the weekly shop without thinking about calorie count. Buy what I fancy not what I think I should eat

Then between those two draw a long squiggly road. This represents the journey between where you are now and where you want to be.

The next thing to do is think about some other points on that line. For example, eventually you want to be going to the gym a couple of times a week. At some stage therefore you will have to go only six days in a week – that is, have a day when you do not go. Once you have thought of another point, think about where on the journey it is. Is it really hard and a big leap from where you are now, so quite near the final destination? Or is it something quite close to where you are now? Maybe it is roughly in the middle. Mark it onto the diagram. You need to keep on doing this until you have a series of points marked, with plenty that are not too far from the start. So think of some things that you could change without it being too terrifying. Maybe you could go to the gym but just do twenty minutes instead one day – and work it down until one day you don't go at all. Mark each of those steps on the diagram. The idea is that you do exactly what the anxiety did – you creep forward – because each little step is not that hard. You may even find you don't notice it too much.

Road diagrams are really helpful in enabling you to take back control from anxiety and stop it from overwhelming you. Each time you take a step forward you are learning that the WCS has not happened after all. And bit by bit you will win back ground from the anxiety and beat back that flame.

9 Some other common problems: self-harm, other addictions and multi-impulsive bulimia

Dealing with an eating disorder is really hard. No matter what people say, it is not simply a case of 'snapping out of it'. We have already talked about some of the things that make it so hard: the anxiety, the difficult thinking patterns, the goals and the drive to push yourself beyond what is possible. However, many people with eating disorders also struggle with other problems. This chapter will look at some of these things, and give some insight into why they are so common among those with eating disorders. However, we cannot do them justice in just one chapter, so if you do struggle with one of these, it is important to seek out some extra help or support.

It is not at all surprising that people struggling with eating disorders sometimes develop other problems. An eating disorder starts in someone desperately trying to find a strategy to cope with difficult feelings, emotions or situations that they otherwise would not know how to handle. But the worst thing about an eating disorder is that although at first it may seem to be the solution, in fact it causes many more problems than it ever solves. On the whole, by the time a sufferer realizes this they are already trapped by the anxiety that an eating disorder triggers, and also by the fact that they know no other way of coping with what their life is throwing at them. The eating disorder therefore continues, but as time goes on, those difficult feelings, emotions and thoughts become more and more troublesome and painful. It is not therefore uncommon for other problems to develop as you desperately attempt to cope with or escape from those feelings.

Self-harm
Self-harm is the act of deliberately injuring yourself physically. As well as becoming increasingly common in general, it is probably the most common problem to find someone struggling with alongside an eating disorder. For most people the harm takes a visible form, such as cutting or burning, but sometimes it can be invisible (like punching yourself somewhere where the bruises will not be visible).

People who self-harm describe how their feelings build up and become gradually more and more overwhelming. This often happens when sufferers are on their own, and is most common in the evenings or at the end of the day when they are tired and more vulnerable (although it can occur at any time of the day). When this happens, feelings that the sufferer has not dealt with engulf them to such an extent that they can think of no way to deal with how bad they are feeling. These feelings can be things that were triggered earlier in the day and might even have happened in the past and not been dealt with. Self-harm is something that people do as a result of feeling this way, in a desperate attempt to feel better. Sufferers often try to stop harming, but talk about how these feelings build up until eventually they are hit at a moment when they cannot think of anything else to do and cannot bear what they are feeling, so harm again. Sometimes self-harm can be very serious, and wounds and injuries frequently require hospital treatment.

Understanding why someone self-harms can be difficult. If you harm yourself, your biggest fear is probably that you do it because there is something wrong with you; that you are weak or deficient in some way or that your brain is wired wrong, meaning you are somehow doomed to feel like this for the rest of your life. On the other hand, if you don't self-harm, it is almost impossible to understand how damaging yourself in some way might help you to feel better.

Be reassured: the vast majority of people who self-harm will eventually stop, either because they work through the way they deal with their emotions and develop more effective coping strategies, or because the situation that triggers the self-harm resolves. The truth is, though, that just like an eating disorder, self-harm is a desperate attempt to find something to do that helps you to regain control when negative and painful emotions take over and seem overwhelming. It is something that can start in normal people who are exposed to extreme levels of stress or negative emotion. The reasons why self-harm develops are still being debated. It is often an expression of the strong emotions that have triggered it. This may be, for example, hitting out at yourself to express a frustration or anger that can be directed nowhere else. When it occurs alongside an eating disorder, self-harm tends to be very closely linked with the feelings and emotions triggered by the eating disorder, and sufferers may specifically harm parts of their body that they feel are fat or unattractive.

Sometimes self-harm can provide a visible illustration of emotional pain, so that the sufferer can validate to themselves just how bad they felt – almost like a reassurance that it really was that bad and they were not overreacting. It can also help them to communicate with someone else just how bad they were feeling when they would find it impossible to put it effectively into words. Sufferers typically struggle tremendously with describing and communicating their feelings, and a wound can portray very powerfully just how bad things were or are.

However, the main theory for self-harm is that sufferers

are harnessing a system that the body uses to cope with injury. When we suffer a serious injury our bodies release hormones called endorphins. These hormones help us to keep calm and make sensible decisions on the spur of the moment. That is why people who have experienced bad accidents often say that they felt amazingly calm and rational straight afterwards. Endorphins really do help us to relax and calm our thinking. Self-harm therefore may be a way of harnessing this system to help people to cope with their feelings.

Self-harm carries with it many problems. Perhaps the greatest of these is that if it does have an effect in reducing emotions and inducing relaxation, this tends to be short term and therefore the next time a need arises, that same desire to harm will be experienced. It does not help sufferers to change their circumstances or to become more able to cope with what they are experiencing. The self-harm itself often becomes very distressing, and the fear that people might find out builds.

Over time self-harm may escalate in a desperate attempt to find a release, and the risk of serious physical injury increases, as well as presenting a long-term issue of coping with the scars that result.

Most sufferers do want to stop harming, and many will try to stop time after time but find they succumb eventually when their tremendous act of will gives way. Self-harm is most likely to respond to therapy and interventions that look at the reason why it occurs, including the emotional cycles that drive and eventually trigger episodes. Self-harm that is linked with an eating disorder often responds very well to treatment for the eating disorder and as someone recovers and starts to generally feel better, the self-harm also resolves.

Self-harm is a very frightening thing to encounter and often people are very scared that it is linked with suicidal feelings or that sufferers are at great risk. On the whole, suicide attempts are quite different from deliberate self-harm, even though they may involve the same actions. Someone who attempts suicide is aiming to end their life, whereas someone who self-harms is trying to cope with theirs. However, it is very important to appreciate that people who self-harm are experiencing some very extreme emotions. This on its own places them at increased risk of struggling with suicidal feelings. Therefore it is vital that someone struggling with self-harm receives help and finds other ways of expressing and dealing with their feelings so that things do not become overwhelming.

DISSOCIATION
Another time that self-harm can become very serious is if it is linked with something called dissociation. Dissociation is something we can all do to some extent, and it describes a state we can slip into where we are not consciously aware of our actions, though we are still awake and functioning apparently normally. Just think of the last time you drove home and realized afterwards that you could not remember most of the journey. However, some people who are exposed to significant trauma, particularly in childhood, can start to dissociate as a way of escaping those feelings. This may become very serious because it can happen without their control, and it means they can slip into periods of time when they are not aware of their actions. Self-harm can be linked with dissociation, either because it triggers a dissociative state as someone separates themselves from the pain (this may also help them to separate from emotional pain and thus be a part of why self-harm is so addictive) or because it brings someone out of a dissociative state – for example, stopping flashbacks or other intrusive memories. Self-harm that takes place in a dissociative state is very serious because wounds and injuries can be severe.

If you or anyone you know is experiencing this kind of self-harm – finding that they were not aware of what they did when they harmed or that they 'lost' a period of time – it is essential that they receive good care and treatment for this as soon as possible.

Other addictions

As well as self-harm, eating disorders are often described – and sometimes treated – alongside other addictions. Whereas an eating disorder is a quite separate kind of addiction, it is not unusual to find some other form of addiction existing alongside an eating disorder. The most common of these is alcohol abuse. This is very serious because eating disorders and substance misuse problems are the two mental health problems associated with the greatest number of deaths, so to be dealing with both at once presents a particularly risky situation.

Just how common it is to struggle with alcoholism if you have an eating disorder is debated, and estimates range from a couple of per cent through to twenty-five per cent (a quarter) of those with anorexia and up to nearly fifty per cent (half) of those struggling with bulimia in one study. Alcohol is often associated with a worsening of symptoms in bulimia, and may trigger episodes of bingeing and purging. Alcohol use is also associated with a higher risk of serious self-harm and suicide attempts. It may also make working on recovery harder and increase the duration or severity of an eating disorder.

Drug use among those with eating disorders, although much less common than alcohol abuse, has also been investigated. Rates vary significantly from study to study, but on the whole we find that they are not greatly different from those you would find in the rest of the population. However, it is certainly true that some people struggle with drug abuse as well as their eating disorder, and often alongside other problems. On the whole this is more commonly seen in people with forms of bulimia than it is in those with anorexia. Drugs that have been reported in studies as sometimes used and abused include marijuana, amphetamines, LSD, Ecstasy and cocaine.

Fighting an eating disorder is never easy, and the existence of another problem or addiction alongside it certainly does not make it any easier. It goes without saying that someone who is fighting both an eating disorder and a significant drug or alcohol problem will need a lot more support as they work towards recovery. They are also likely to need specific input targeting this other addiction as well as the eating disorder. However, treatment for one problem will not be distinct and separate from therapy for another, and it is likely that the process of recovery and self-discovery involved will help to work on both issues.

A special note

One issue that merits specific mention in this chapter is the current debate over a condition called **multi-impulsive bulimia**. Multi-impulsive bulimia was first named in the early 1990s when a research study looked at a particular group of patients with bulimia. Another study went on to describe this sub-group of sufferers in more detail, stating that someone suffering with bulimia who also showed elements of three or more 'impulsive' behaviours (including self-harm and drug or alcohol abuse) fitted into this group of patients who also seemed to struggle particularly with the usual treatment regimes for bulimia.

Exactly whether or not multi-impulsive bulimia is in a separate diagnostic category to 'normal' bulimia is hotly debated, as is what proportion of those suffering with bulimia could be placed within this category – and in some ways neither of these things matters. What is important once again is that people struggling with other impulsive kinds of behaviour as well as bulimia are likely to need greater support as they work on recovery. They may struggle more than others with issues of anxiety, and may also need help to deal with past trauma or abuse.

Part 3

Planning your route

Starting out on the path to recovery

10 What is recovery and is it possible?

This is a question that anyone struggling against an eating disorder will have asked – perhaps with fear, or perhaps with anticipation of what they can look forward to. Recovery is something you might hear other people talking about a lot. They want you to recover – they want you to work towards recovery – and it is something that they are often placing all their hopes on.

If you are the sufferer, this can leave you feeling under a huge amount of pressure. And it is made even harder by the fact that having a clear idea of what recovery will be like is very difficult when you are in the midst of an eating disorder. In fact many people end up in treatment without ever really thinking about what recovery is. This is a bit like leaving your house in London with a vague idea of going to Edinburgh, but without any idea of where that is or how you will get there. It is not that you won't get there this way, but it would be much better to think about your route before you start out.

This is what one person who has recovered from anorexia has to say about her experiences of recovery:

'Recovering from my eating disorder was a bit of a journey into the unknown. I didn't really know what to expect… One of the hardest things, I think, was facing those moments when life does get hard – probably just normal things. Because at first I was so excited by how everything was finally changing for the better and all I was achieving. But then there wasn't so much new to achieve – or nothing so easy anyway. Constantly having

to be willing to challenge who I was and how I reacted was really hard. And if I ever got low or upset or fed up – or if anything went wrong – I used to be really scared that it was some kind of "sign" that I was doomed to never get over this completely. I think some of those times were made much harder by my own tendency to go off at the deep end the minute the "rosy" feelings went away. I didn't know what was normal and I didn't know anyone else who had recovered to ask.'

Of course the most important reason for knowing your route before setting out on a journey is to try to avoid getting lost. Ultimately the biggest fear of most people who are thinking about fighting an eating disorder is that they will end up at something that is not real recovery. Many people fear, for example, that recovery will be about being fatter but still feeling the same – so in fact feeling worse. Or they are afraid of trying to get over one eating disorder and ending up with another.

Some people may have already experienced this, and statistically people with anorexia nervosa risk developing bulimia nervosa eventually if they do not start to move towards recovery. This is simply because very few people can keep up the required degree of control in overriding their body's natural impulse to eat. If you have already experienced slipping out of one eating disorder into another, this makes thinking about recovery very painful.

Another thing that makes thinking about recovery hard is if you have experienced some degree of recovery before but relapsed. This experience is very common. Some studies suggest that as many as a quarter of those who have had hospital treatment for anorexia will experience some form of relapse within twelve months of discharge. Meanwhile a lot of people with bulimia will have tried to stop and change their eating behaviour, sometimes many times. However, as we have discussed earlier, the way in which they do that means they are setting themselves up to fail – and they are likely to slip back into the binge-purge-diet cycle again. So all in all, many sufferers feel that they have already failed at recovery – meaning that they fear failing again, or even that they worry they will never be able to get over this.

One of the most horrendous things an eating disorder does to people is to rob them of hope. This can affect sufferers, their families and, in some cases, even the professionals working with them. The truth is, though, that recovery *is* possible. It is not easy, and for some people it may take a long time, but it is possible. Before we look at what the experience of recovery is really like, let's take a few moments to think a bit more about the concept of recovery.

What does recovery mean to you?

Whether you yourself are suffering or you are supporting someone else, join me in thinking about what exactly recovery means to you. Stop reading this, find a pen and some paper, and have a go at writing your own list of what recovery is (or will be) for you or the person you are supporting. Perhaps you could make two lists, and consider what *is* included in recovery and what definitely *isn't* part of recovery. What are the signs that someone is or is not recovered?

Remember, recovery is about getting to the place where you are free and happy. You may have had some experiences of treatment for eating disorders that you feel do not focus on a real or full recovery. If this is the case, then make sure you write down what you think does focus on this.

When you have finished, have a look at the lists on the following pages, which were put together by a group of people on a weekend looking at recovery. Most were people who had themselves recovered, so they really should have known what they were talking about. Have a look and see how many things you agree with.

RECOVERY IS:

- Freedom – from shame/guilt, from obsessive thoughts, from the need to achieve
- Confidence
- Eating/food no longer an issue
- Balance – sometimes eating too much, sometimes too little, but not thrown back into eating disorder
- Being different
- Letting go/finding a new identity
- Being able to enjoy food as a pleasure
- Opportunity
- Wider perspective
- Having family
- Building up self-esteem and self-acceptance
- Able to eat 'nice' foods without fear of losing control
- Dignity
- Restoring perspective
- Having no fear
- Relief
- A challenge
- Being able to see yourself as you really are
- Moving on
- More fun
- Not a substituted shackle – it is having no shackles
- Looking to the future
- Letting go of the illness
- Freedom from being trapped
- Acceptance of yourself

- Not being too hard on yourself
- Peace of mind
- Not being alone
- Accepting the things you cannot change
- Letting go of the past
- Having new thoughts – not staying trapped or static
- Being able to give enough to yourself and as a result the best of yourself to others
- Admittance
- Being honest and true to yourself and others
- Handing over the uncontrollable to your higher power
- Change
- Being selfless
- Doing the right things
- Not taking things out on yourself when things go wrong
- Feeling you deserve recovery

RECOVERY IS NOT:
- Diets all the time
- Being chained to something else
- Just gaining weight
- Papering over the cracks
- Constant denial/keeping busy so you don't feel bad
- A magic wand (it isn't instant relief)
- Never having any problems ever again (it is about dealing with them in a more positive way)
- Denial
- Isolation

- Dishonesty
- Living in the past
- Dwelling on the past
- Ignoring your 'inner self'
- Revisiting previous habits
- Living a lie
- Harbouring bitterness
- Turning anger in on yourself
- Guilt
- Starvation
- Depending too much on others
- Losing responsibility
- Fear
- Restriction
- A 'hamster wheel' of activity

So how did your lists compare? If they were very different, then this is something you need to work on some more – perhaps with a therapist or with your GP, or even just by chatting it over with friends or family. You might like to ask some other people to make their own lists and compare them with yours – and with these.

The overriding message from these lists is that recovery is actually about *gain, not pain*. Yes, recovery involves dealing with difficult emotions and sometimes painful issues from your past, but it is about finally being free from them.

Compare the lists above with the next one – written by someone who had been struggling with anorexia for many years.

RECOVERY WILL BE:

- Going back to feeling depressed all the time
- Looking awful in clothes
- Feeling very self-conscious and vulnerable without having any tools to defend myself
- Returning to the old me – bad, stupid, clumsy, second rate, odd
- Keeping the friendships I have now
- Being able to do more things
- Going back to being out of control
- Not knowing who I am any more
- Going back to being invisible and not knowing how to communicate how I am feeling
- Having to seem to be happy all the time
- Not being able to show my real feelings
- Losing the real me
- Being ugly and fat
- Failing

Do you see why having a clear concept of recovery is so important? This person had spent a long time trying to work towards recovery and was coming up against a brick wall. She desperately wanted to be able to meet the targets being set for her, but her concept of recovery was all wrong. And who would honestly want to work towards the destination she thought she was headed for?

The reality of recovery

So what is it *really* like to work towards recovery? One of the great things I have found about working for Anorexia & Bulimia Care (see page 144) is that I get to meet many people who have recovered from eating disorders. I have

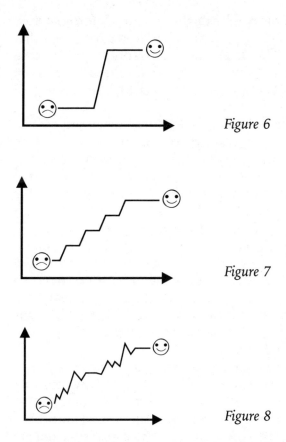

Figure 6

Figure 7

Figure 8

heard lots of stories, read lots of testimonies and seen lots of lives change dramatically for the better. And all the stories I hear have certain things in common.

Take a look at the graph in Figure 6, which represents what many people think recovery will be like. They think there will be a period of time when the sufferer is ill and unhappy, and this will last for a while. Then there will be a time of rapid change, when they start to get better. Their health and mood will improve steadily until they enter phase three, when they are healthy and happy.

This sounds nice and straightforward. Unfortunately it is also a very unusual pattern to see in recovery. So what about Figure 7? This is another illustration of what some people think recovery will be like. Again there is an initial period of illness and a final time when the person is well and recovered. This time the gap in between is not so smooth – a jagged uphill struggle with some periods of fast improvement and others where improvement is much slower. This is much closer to what real recovery is like, but it still isn't very accurate. You see, even in this example, the period where recovery is 'in process' is a time when things are always 'on the up'.

If you talk to those who have recovered, they will describe an experience much more like Figure 8. This shows the reality: recovery is about ups *and* downs – sometimes periods of time that involve a decline in health or how the sufferer feels emotionally. Some of these times may look like total relapse. Steps forward are often followed by steps back, and the path is very unpredictable, even though over time it does move forward.

I said earlier that most people's biggest fear is that they will never experience true recovery. This is why knowing that some 'downs' are a normal part of recovery is so important. Lots of people cope OK with recovery until they hit one of these. Then they plunge into a depression and are overwhelmed by fear. They feel that any improvement they had seen up until then was just a fake – an illusion. And hopelessness comes flooding back.

But the truth is that it took many months and years to develop an eating disorder and the (false) beliefs and rules that sustain it. You can't expect all those to disappear just like that. Every time there is a slip, this is a chance to learn from it something else that needs to be worked through for true recovery to be achieved. So these times are not failures. They are vital *opportunities* on the road to recovery.

Think of a child learning to walk. Children fall over all the time. Recently my toddler daughter fell over and bruised her forehead and nose. Two weeks later it had healed, but then she did exactly the same thing again. Today, however, she fell in the same way, but this time she got her hands out in time to catch herself. So each time she fell she learned from it and eventually she will be steady enough on her feet that the idea of falling over seems ridiculous. Recovery is much the same.

Two people's experience of recovery

I will leave the final word in this chapter to two people I have known and worked with who have walked the path to recovery.

First we hear from Beth, aged twenty, recovering from anorexia nervosa:

'What did I used to think of recovery? Quite simply I thought I could never get there. I was trapped in this dark unhappy world and I really could see no way out. I couldn't see where to start, or how I could possibly do it. I couldn't imagine myself leading a life like other people. I could never see myself sitting down to eat a meal like other people, eating what they eat, and not being totally petrified.

'What about now? Well, a lot has changed and I am now "recovering" I think. And I'm learning it's a long process! My feelings on recovery have changed a lot too. I guess as I worked through things in my past and feelings about myself etc. I gradually started to see things a different way and occasionally I found myself with a small amount of determination to fight and beat this. I started to get small glimpses of the light at the end of the tunnel – just a fleeting feeling that this is possible. That was all I needed. I could see that freedom was there and attainable. That feeling, knowing I'm getting further towards the end and further away from it is hard to describe. It's a

deep feeling of great joy. I can't really describe it properly! Recovery for me is very much a "two steps forward, one step back" process, but the important thing is that I am finally heading in the right direction, and freedom is where my aim lies. Sometimes it is hard to keep my eyes on where I am heading and I risk slipping back into the old thought patterns and the old way of life. So far I have managed to get back on track slowly if I slip off and lose focus for a while. I've got a long way to go, but I always hold on to the fact I know freedom can ultimately be mine. I am learning that it is OK to have bad days. It doesn't mean everything's a disaster.

'There are definitely two sides to recovery. Yes, it is terrifying, it really is. I'm not denying that. Learning to eat, risking being kind to yourself? It's overwhelming and I have days where I just don't know what to do with myself. It can be slow and painful, and I'm constantly having to try to reassure myself of things that I am sometimes not actually really convinced of yet. Learning to eat and balance meals is very difficult. For me it was just starting to eat at three mealtimes a day to begin with. I've found that as I've stuck to trying things again and again, they get easier (things like eating certain foods, wearing clothes that fit, etc.).

'Recovery is frightening but worth it. It is the best move you can make; the most important and life-changing decision. And it changes your life for the better.

'Recovery involves taking risks, it takes courage and determination, but as you get better, these things also grow so that you are able to cope with the next stage. I have become braver as I have discovered that things aren't as bad as they seemed – eating hasn't ruined my life, but rather is improving it. I've come a long way already and although I feel there is still a long way to go and it's hard, I know in my life now there is much more that is positive. As you recover you start to feel real happiness – better than any you can get from starving or losing weight because it is real. It's amazing as you start feeling it.

'The best things about recovery are:

• *Amazement as you realize "forbidden" foods are actually allowed, and waking up the next day to discover they really haven't done anything bad to you.*

• *Smiling much more. The ability to feel happy, laughing and joking and gradually having more energy to actually live.*

• *Sometimes walking down the street and feeling good about myself. I'm not saying it happens all the time, but I started to have moments, and then those moments started to become longer, and I am feeling OK with myself most of the time now, and that brings such an amazing feeling with it, gradually realizing that maybe, just maybe, you're OK (acceptable).*

• *Energy to get through the day and not be so exhausted. Has to be a plus side.*

• *Improved relationships – proper relationships. Being able to love and be loved (friends, siblings, parents, etc.).*

• *So much less paranoia – knowing people really do like me.*

• *More sleep.'*

And this is Dawn, thirty-five, recovered from bulimia:

'I can't remember ever having a normal relationship with food or with my body image. One of my first memories is being in a shop with my mum and one of her friends commenting on how "big" I was. Home life was always stressful, chaotic and difficult. Arguments and violence were the norm. I learned to take comfort in food at an early age.

'During my teenage years I began to feel deeply unhappy with my appearance. I felt I should weigh seven stone and was repulsed and frustrated at my nine-stone frame. I started dieting and joined a slimming club. Looking back I can remember the feeling that I was not acceptable unless I could reach this weight. My life was on hold. The only time I felt worth was when the scales registered more pounds lost.

'I ate less and less, and then one day I was walking home and I don't know why, or if there was any specific reason, but I walked into the corner shop and bought numerous bars of chocolate. I went home and ate them so fast I could barely taste them. I felt out of control but exhilarated for a few moments, then suddenly I was plunged into a guilty despair and had to get rid of the food. The compulsion to vomit was as strong as the desire to binge. Once I felt I had got all the food out, I felt exhausted and disgusted, and vowed I would never do that again. I was fifteen and that was the start of eighteen years of bulimia.

'For many years I convinced myself I had control over it. I wouldn't have even believed I had an eating disorder. Each episode ended with me being determined and promising myself that I would resist the urge to binge next time, eat less, never eat anything containing sugar, or white flour, or fat... The list of foods I banned for myself grew year on year. I think I did this because they were the foods that if I ate one bite of would lead to a binge. But even with all my "rules" the binges continued, and so did the desire to compensate for them. Sometimes I would exercise for hours. I was once told to leave the gym by one of the supervisors who had been watching me. I would also do 600-calorie days to counteract a binge, as well as vomiting and eventually taking laxatives.

'Something changed in my late twenties. My life had settled down, I had escaped a very abusive and violent marriage with a man who had numerous affairs. This only reinforced my belief that I was worthless, less than hopeless.

I met my second husband Jon and we were happy. He was kind and supportive, and showed me love and affection. I had no need of the bulimia any more. I wanted to stop it, but I couldn't. Sometimes I would manage three days of near normality with food, but then I would slip and be hiding wrappers in the utility room again and trying to vomit in silence. I remember Jon coming home one day and interrupting a binge. I felt so angry with him. It was irrational, powerful anger and when it subsided I knew I had to tell him, which I eventually did. Even though the bulimia continued, I had taken a big step. I realized I didn't want to live like this any more and I had told someone about it.

'I began to search for an answer. I looked on the internet and read some books, but I just became more and more depressed and desperate. Many times I thought I was making progress, but then I would slip back into old behaviour and feel worse than ever. One day I was bingeing and searching the internet for advice and I came across the ABC website. I rang the number and spoke to someone. This turned out to be an amazing support. In my early days of recovery I would ring very often. With encouragement from this, I went to my GP and I found out there was a new bulimia clinic just started in a hospital near me, and I asked to be referred there. I also accepted anti-depressants. I was so low it was hard to function. My mind thought about food constantly, either planning it or analysing it. At this point the bulimia was still there, but I was trying to fight it and follow the advice in recommended books.

'I waited nine months for my first appointment. From day one of the treatment I knew I was going to overcome this illness that had robbed me of so much. I desperately wanted it to stop. I wanted to get better.

'The treatment was a cognitive behavioural therapy approach. I had food diaries to fill in after every meal or snack. I had to eat six times a day, which was incredibly hard. Gradually we introduced more and more foods from my banned

list. I began to feel connections between my emotions and my desire to binge. I also began to stop saying yes to everyone, to set boundaries and to take some time to do things for enjoyment. My initial assessment score put me in the range of severe eating disorder. After nine months I was in the range of normal. I had begun to accept myself and make the most of my appearance. I was sleeping well, totally off anti-depressants, eating a wide, varied diet, and enjoying my life with my husband and children. My weight was stable for the first time in my adult life.

'That was June 2004 and I have been free from bulimia ever since. I love my life now. I have so much energy. I enjoy food and exercise. I look forward to the future and I no longer despise the person I see in the mirror. I have a full life and food is only part of it. It is wonderful to be free from bulimia. It robbed me of so much all those years and I believed things about myself that were not true. I have now applied to be a befriender for ABC. I want to support others and help them to get free from this illness.'

11 How to get help and handle treatment

Living with an eating disorder is incredibly hard. Whether it is you or someone you love who is suffering, the strain of dealing with mealtimes, weight gain or loss and the constant risk of physical problems caused by the eating disorder means that life can feel like a rollercoaster. However, if there is one thing more frightening than the illness for a sufferer, it is seeking help and treatment.

Seeking help can be frightening

There are two main reasons for this. The first one is to do with the illusion an eating disorder paints: that the sufferer is in control. Most eating disorders start off with someone desperately trying to take control of one thing in their world: their weight. But the sad truth is that an eating disorder is not about being in control at all, and at some stage the disorder itself takes over and it is the anxiety that controls the sufferer. Seeking treatment means that someone is admitting to some degree that this has happened – that they need some help to get out of the situation in which they have found themselves. This is very hard because the whole point for them was to take control and now they have to admit they have lost it completely.

The second reason seeking treatment is so hard is because it involves letting go of some of the secrecy involved in the eating disorder and potentially handing over control to someone else. Most people with eating disorders keep a large part of their behaviour hidden or secret – partly due to shame and guilt about what they are doing, but also partly because if no one knows about it then no one can stop them. Seeking treatment means potentially having to share with someone else what has been going on, and therefore losing the protection that secrecy has previously given them.

Going to see your GP

For most people the first port of call in seeking help will be their GP. On the whole it is your GP who will co-ordinate whatever treatment you receive and should keep an eye on what is going on and how you are doing. This places quite a lot of responsibility on the GP's shoulders, so do think about who this should be when you make your appointment. This is probably not the time to accept the appointment with a locum GP you have never heard of before. Try to get an appointment with the doctor you usually see – someone you like and feel reasonably at ease with, if possible. This is also not the time to have one of the five-minute 'emergency' appointments many surgeries give out at short notice. The best thing to do is ask for a double appointment so that you have time to talk things over with the doctor, and most surgeries will allow you to book something in this way.

Of course, once you have booked your appointment and turned up at the specified time, you need to communicate successfully to the doctor what has been going on. But this is easier said than done. By the time you get into the surgery you will probably have gone over the appointment again and again in your head. What will the doctor say? What will you say? What will happen? All those anxieties will probably rush over you when you walk into the room, so to make sure you do manage to get everything you need to say across, it is probably best to write down some bullet points before going in.

But what about actually getting to the appointment in

the first place? If there is a chance you won't be able to go through with it because you are so scared, why not think about taking a friend with you? This also has the advantage that your friend can speak for you if you find it hard to get words out once you are there. Or, if you know you will find it hard to tell the doctor face to face what is going on, you could write a letter and post it so that your doctor gets it before your appointment (best give them a few days before your appointment to read the letter to make sure they have had time). That way you go into an appointment knowing that in a sense the worst is over. Remember, you need to do whatever you can to help yourself get over this hard step so that you can start to take back control from the eating disorder and *remain* in control.

What is your GP likely to do?

So what is your GP likely to do once you have admitted what has been going on? Well, some of the things GPs *don't* do might surprise you more than what they do do! For example, very often they will not do very much at first. They might discuss some options with you and do some simple medical checks, such as blood pressure, and then they may suggest that you come back in a couple of weeks to see how things are going. Sometimes this can be really frustrating, particularly if you are a friend or family member and had been desperately hoping something would be done straight away. But this is often due to a GP not wanting to act without the agreement of a sufferer, and if they are aware of how scary this all is to someone suffering, they might take this approach to ensure that their patient does not feel too overwhelmed.

One thing people always want to know is whether their GP will weigh them. Some will and some will not. You do have the right to refuse to be weighed, but the reality is that they need to have some idea of your weight so that they know what the risk is of your being physically ill because of the eating disorder. They also might want to keep an eye on how your weight changes in order to get an idea of how serious things are and how gently they can move things along. You do not, however, have to know yourself what your weight is. If you would prefer not to know, look away while you are weighed and ask the doctor not to tell you how much you weigh. Try not to read too much into anything the doctor says about weight. For example, if they don't want to weigh you this does not mean you must look fat. It may simply mean that they do not want to push you too hard this time and know that being weighed would be very difficult.

Concerns people have about seeing their GP
Plucking up the courage to go to visit the GP can be very hard. Here are the top three fears and concerns people often have:

1. THE DOCTOR WILL MAKE ME EAT OR WILL TAKE CONTROL
Probably the biggest fear of anyone struggling with an eating disorder is that the minute they admit what is going on, someone will take control from them and force them to eat certain things or in a certain way, or stop them from purging, exercising, and so on.

The truth is that this is very unlikely to happen. Even in circumstances where someone is physically very ill, most GPs will try to find some kind of compromise or first step that the person suffering can agree to. This is because time and time again, research has shown that treatment has a much better chance of being effective if it is not done against someone's will. The most important thing to remember is that if *you* seek treatment, *you* are in control.

So many times I have seen people struggling,

particularly with anorexia, who are so scared of having to go into hospital that they avoid seeking help and put it off. Meanwhile they get so unwell they eventually collapse. When this happens, very often they have to be admitted to hospital there and then for treatment, without any time to prepare or come to terms with what has to happen. This kind of admission is also very rarely to a specialist eating disorders ward, or even a mental health ward. Usually it is to a general medical ward where staff can care for someone physically frail and unwell. This can make it even more traumatic for everyone involved.

Recent guidelines for treating eating disorders recommend that where possible treatment is received as an out-patient. So if you seek help early enough, the chances are you will be able to remain at home while you are being treated. Although seeking treatment may be scary, at least you are in control of what happens next and you are allowing yourself the time to think about what you want to do and to decide what happens next.

2. THE DOCTOR WILL NOT THINK I AM THIN ENOUGH TO HAVE AN EATING DISORDER

As I have already mentioned, this is a common fear of people struggling with eating disorders. Unfortunately it is one of the features of an eating disorder that people think they are overweight, even if they are in fact not. Because the stereotype of someone with an eating disorder is someone who is very thin, they then find it impossible to admit that they have an eating disorder. The reality is, whether you really are thin or not, an eating disorder is about much more than what you weigh, and in fact most people with eating disorders are normal weight or overweight.

Remember, the most important thing is how this is making you *feel*. So try not to get caught in the trap of worrying that you are not thin enough to have an eating disorder. Think about getting a friend or family member you can chat this over with and who can help you take this step of talking things through with your GP.

3. THE DOCTOR WILL NOT TAKE ME SERIOUSLY

It is not unusual for people to find it takes some time for their GP to start to take action and to diagnose an eating disorder. However, this is not necessarily because they are not taking things seriously. Often it is because they do not want to jump to conclusions, and eating disorders are hard to diagnose 'on the spot' in one appointment. It may be obvious to you what is going on if you live with a sufferer, but it is not so simple from your GP's perspective. Remember too that they may appear to be taking things lightly, when in fact they are simply being careful and not wanting to rush someone into taking action.

Sometimes, however, it can be more than this. In cases where the sufferer is much younger (say, under fourteen), older (over thirty) or is male, eating disorders can be the last thing on a GP's mind as they seek to rule out all kinds of other problems first. Or, if they have not had much experience of eating disorders, it may not be something that jumps to their mind, particularly if they are busy. If you, as the sufferer, or as a carer or friend, are convinced it is an eating disorder, do mention this to the GP and explain why you are worried. Do not assume that they will pick up hints, or guess what is going on.

If your GP remains unsympathetic, or does not seem to be taking you seriously, you can always consider seeing another GP at the same surgery. Or do call one of the eating disorders charities for further advice (see numbers at the end of this book). Most of all, though, do not blame yourself if things do not go according to plan, particularly if something is said that is unhelpful or even hurtful. GPs are expected to have a wealth of knowledge and experience of everything, and it isn't your fault if they have not actually dealt with eating disorders before.

What to expect from your GP

Whatever happens when you go to your GP, there are certain things you can and should expect about the way you are treated. The NICE (National Institute of Clinical Excellence) guidelines for the treatment of eating disorders (published in February 2004)[5] state that whatever happens, all treatment should be supportive, non-judgmental and confidential. You can expect your GP to take your concerns seriously, and to put the time into checking them out. You should be treated in an understanding and sympathetic manner.

The NICE guidelines emphasize the importance of the GP in co-ordinating treatment for eating disorders, and GPs are encouraged to try to catch them as early as possible, including carrying out screening tests where there is a suspicion that an eating disorder might be present. This means that your GP should take your concerns seriously, even if you or the person you are concerned about are only in the early stages of an eating disorder.

What next?

If the GP feels that there is indeed something going on which looks like an eating disorder, the chances are that the sufferer will then be referred for further help. In fact about four out of five cases of anorexia and three out of five of bulimia are referred on to more specialist care – usually to psychiatrists of some kind. So you will probably

[5] See C59, pub 2004. 'Eating Disorders: Anorexia Nervosa, Bulimia Nervosa and Related Eating Disorders', *Understanding NICE Guidance: a Guide for People with Eating Disorders, their Advocates and Carers, and the Public*. To order copies call 0870 1555 455 and quote reference number N0407. A version in English and Welsh is also available: quote reference N0408.

be told by the GP that you are being referred, and you will then have to wait for a letter to come from the specialist centre inviting you to come for an appointment. This may be a specialist treatment centre for eating disorders, or it may be a general psychiatrist or, for those under eighteen, a unit specializing in treating child and adolescent mental health problems. What treatment you are offered will depend largely on where you live, although in some cases you may be offered the chance to travel further afield for specialist care.

There are a lot of different approaches available to treat eating disorders. Some may be offered on the NHS, some in private units, and still others by private counsellors or other therapists. Perhaps more than the specific kind of intervention, by far the most important thing is that the sufferer finds someone they feel able to relate to and work with.

This is perhaps the most crucial stage of finding treatment, so here are some of the common questions people ask, together with some suggestions and solutions:

WHAT IF I AM JUST PUT ON A LONG WAITING LIST?
It is a well-documented fact that eating disorders services in the UK are highly oversubscribed. Unfortunately, that means you might have to wait for some time to receive treatment. Most centres will give you an initial assessment appointment without too long a wait, but then there may be a longer wait to be assigned to someone to treat you.

It is important to remember that if you are waiting to be seen, this does not mean there is nothing you can do in the meantime. Neither does it mean that your eating disorder is not serious enough to be treated. You might want to pursue getting some private counselling or support – call one of the eating disorders helplines for further advice on how to do this. Do also return to your GP to discuss what has happened and what your options are. There may be a counsellor or dietician attached to the surgery whom you could see, or at the very least you might be able to have a regular appointment with your GP or the practice nurse so that you are getting some support and someone is keeping an eye on how things are going. The main thing is that you do not slip into despair just because you are on a waiting list.

WHAT IF I DON'T LIKE THE PERSON I AM REFERRED TO?
This is a fairly common problem. Fighting an eating disorder is a bit like being in a war, and because the sufferer is so scared of losing control (or having it taken from them), everyone who tries to help them seems at first to be an enemy. It is easy for sufferers to feel as though everyone else is fighting against them.

If you are referred to someone – a psychologist, a psychiatrist, a counsellor or someone else – try to give them a chance. Be aware that you may make instant judgments about them and because you are feeling so stressed out and scared you might be too harsh on them. Sometimes simple things can make you feel that you dislike them – for example, their age, how they dress, or the way they talk to you. But remember, they are actually trying to help you feel better. Just as it is important for them to take the time to get to know you, it is important that you give them a chance and don't assume you will not like them.

If there is something specific you would like some help with, then do ask them. Perhaps they are focusing on your eating and in fact you would like some help with trying to handle the anxiety. Or maybe they want to talk about the thoughts that are behind the eating disorder when you want to think about what recovery is. Whatever it is, if you are proactive and discuss things with them, you will get a lot more out of treatment.

WHAT ABOUT MEDICATION?

For most sufferers the issue of taking medication produces mixed feelings. Using medication to treat eating disorders is not most people's first choice, but there certainly is evidence that it can help, both in calming and controlling what is happening in the short term, and in helping to reduce anxiety and obsessive thinking. It has also been shown that some anti-depressants can reduce the frequency of binge–purge cycles in bulimia. Drug treatment can also help to lighten mood and reduce obsessive thinking so that it is much easier for someone to engage with therapy and be able to work through things at a deeper level. It may also help you to cope while you are on a waiting list for further treatment.

On the whole, however, medication alone is not a sufficient treatment for most people with eating disorders, and some form of psychological or 'talking' therapy is usually required alongside drug treatment. If it is suggested to you that medication might help and you are worried, do talk this through with whoever is treating you, or with your GP.

WHAT IF I AM ADMITTED TO HOSPITAL IN AN EMERGENCY?

As I have already mentioned, this can be one of the most traumatic ways to have to face treatment, but it is not unusual at all, particularly for those fighting anorexia. Because of the impact anorexia has on your physical health – and because it is often very hard for people to seek help – it can get to the stage where the eating disorder can mean you are critically ill and even at risk of death. Sadly people do die from anorexia, so do not take this lightly. You may think that you are not thin enough to be that ill, but that is what the eating disorder tells you and is part of the illness. If things get this bad, then a spell in hospital may be required to stabilize you physically before you can have any other treatment, or you may be admitted because you have collapsed and been taken to A & E. It can get so serious that even if you do not want to go into hospital, you might have to – either because you are sectioned under the Mental Health Act (this is a law which means that if you are not able to understand how ill you are, and therefore refuse treatment, you can be forced to have treatment if your life is actually at risk) or because you are under sixteen and your parents consent to you being treated.

If this has happened to you and you are reading this book in hospital, I know that this is probably a really difficult time for you. If you are ill enough to have been admitted as an emergency, you are likely to be on a general medical ward. This means that there is serious concern for your health and you may need to have a nasogastric tube put in, or be put on bed-rest. Remember that these measures are only to protect you. Even though they may trigger that terror of putting on weight, they are not designed to make you fat – just to try to protect you from the very real risk that you might lose your life to your eating disorder. If your weight is very low, and/or you are dehydrated, you will find it hard to think things through clearly and make decisions about your future. The nasogastric tube should help with this too. The sooner you are able to help yourself by eating a little and drinking enough fluid, this can be stopped.

The best advice to you, should you find yourself in this position, is to use this opportunity to think really carefully about what you want for your future. The fact that you are in hospital means that your future is in very serious jeopardy. If you haven't already done so, read Chapter 5 and work through the suggested exercises. Think about the things you want to live for – the things in your future you are hoping for, or the events and things you want to see. Those are the reasons why in the short term you want to survive this fight. Perhaps write a couple of these things down and put them somewhere you can see them to remind you why you want to fight back and not lose your life.

Talk to the medical staff about how you are feeling and what is happening to you. It can be very difficult to find someone with the time to talk to you, but if you do find someone you feel you can trust, take the opportunity to talk to them. It may be that the staff taking care of you have never looked after someone with anorexia before, so be prepared to explain to them just how hard this is for you, and work with them so that you can cope better with the treatment you need.

Finally, do ask if you can be transferred to a specialist treatment centre, particularly if you are told that you will need to have a nasogastric tube put in. The NICE guidelines for treating eating disorders state that this kind of 're-feeding' should only be done in a specialist setting, where staff have the experience and skills required for such a difficult and potentially traumatic treatment. So it is important to talk to those caring for you about this.

12 About food and eating

Considering that this is a book about eating disorders, it may surprise you that I have not actually mentioned food and eating until nearly the last chapter. This is quite deliberate because although you may have come to this book wanting help with your eating patterns, or those of someone you care for, the root of eating disorders is actually far from food and eating. Recovery too is about much more than just what you do or do not eat. That is why I have talked about those subjects first. However, there does come a time when it is helpful to look at the issues surrounding eating and how to handle changing your eating habits, and this chapter will look briefly at some of the issues you might come across.

What is 'normal' eating?

Ultimately, the main aim when working on recovery from an eating disorder is to return to 'normal' eating. However, this may be tricky for two reasons. The first is that it may be hard to know what normal eating actually is. Many people are caught up in their own cycles of unhelpful eating behaviour – maybe nothing as bad as a full-blown eating disorder, but not healthy food relationships. We receive so many messages about eating these days – from the media, the government, the shops we buy our food from… and all this can make it hard to work out what is actually normal.

The second reason why this can be hard is that you might never have actually eaten 'normally'. Lots of people who have developed an eating disorder will have a long-term history of a troubled relationship with food, perhaps comfort eating or dieting a lot when they were younger. Recovery is not about returning to this kind of lifestyle. It is about learning a relationship with food that is healthy, both physically and psychologically.

Normal eating is ultimately about five things:

1. No food is forbidden. This means that all kinds of foods are eaten and enjoyed – admittedly some not as often as others.

2. Not being obsessive. There are no strict lists of foods, nor is food weighed or counted. Whereas normal eating might mean trying to stick to guidelines such as eating five fruit or vegetables a day, this does not become obsessive; nor does it cause anxiety.

3. Sometimes eating too much, sometimes too little. Normal eating does not mean we count or calculate what we eat. It means that we eat according to our real appetite (not emotional appetite) every day, and trust our body to work out the difference.

4. Not being chained to the scales. Normal eating does not mean weighing yourself every day, or being obsessed with what your weight is. Normal eating is about having an instinctive (and roughly accurate) idea of where your weight is and adjusting your eating accordingly.

5. Not dieting. Normal eating is not about being on a constant diet. It might be about trying to eat healthily and following guidelines, but it has a freedom about it which inevitably means that on some days you will break all the rules, but that is OK!

For many people, the biggest fear surrounding normal eating is allowing themselves to listen to their natural appetite and let go of the strict control they have around food. For them eating 'normally' is dominated by the fear of losing control, of overeating and getting fat.

It is important to remember that if your body is in a state of starvation, it will be craving food, and you can be in that position without being desperately underweight if you have been restricting your eating. If your body is deficient in certain vitamins, minerals and other essential elements of a healthy diet (and this can happen even if you are overweight if your diet is poor), you may start to crave food (see Chapter 2). In part this is responsible for the terrifying urge that people experience at first when they do begin to eat properly again which makes them feel that they could just eat and eat and eat. This feeling often holds people back from starting to eat normally, but the truth is that continuing to restrict only makes the urge stronger. The only way to overcome it is to eat normally, replenishing your body's stores so that it does not need to seek food constantly. So do not be afraid that normal eating involves dealing with that urge day to day – it does not. It will pass and leave you able to eat without the accompanying obsessive thinking that can make life so exhausting.

How to handle starting to change your eating habits

If you are wanting to change your eating habits – either on your own or with the support of a therapist – there are a couple of really important things to do.

The first is to make sure that your GP knows what you are doing and is supporting you in this. This is partly so that you have that extra avenue of encouragement but also so that she or he can keep an eye on your physical health and how you are getting on. It may be that if you get to a stage where you decide not to weigh yourself any more the GP can weigh you periodically (without telling you the weight) and therefore make sure that you are not gaining or losing too much weight.

The second thing is to find someone you will see more regularly – a friend or family member perhaps – who knows what you are doing and again can provide support. That may be practical support such as promising to make sure you do not lose control and eat too much, menu planning or helping you go to the supermarket and choose food. Do also think about getting some professional support with working on your eating. Your GP may be able to refer you to a dietician, or you may be able to discuss healthy eating with the practice nurse.

Whatever the eating disorder you are recovering from, inevitably what you are going to need to try to do is improve your daily eating. If you have struggled with binge-eating episodes, then eating regular, adequate meals will help you to avoid the urge to binge again. If you have been fighting anorexia, you will need to start to add foods back into your diet. In both cases, though, you will be doing two of the same things: learning what normal meals are and facing previously forbidden or frightening foods.

LEARNING ABOUT WHAT NORMAL MEALS ARE
It is important that as you improve your diet, you also work towards eating normal, regular meals. Eating like this will decrease the chances of your body craving food and therefore decrease the risk of you slipping out of control. In time, this will also help to reduce and eventually stop the obsessive thoughts about food that probably plague you at the moment. Normal eating is about eating three meals a day, and probably snacking occasionally between meals. It does not mean

following a diet plan, but inevitably at first you might find it helpful to plan with someone what you are going to eat.

As a first step in this process, you will find it helpful to get some snapshots of what normal eating really is. Think of a few friends who you know have a pretty healthy relationship with food and ask them to keep a diary for a few days of what they eat, when they eat it and why. This might be a bit scary for you, but if you can explain to them why this will be helpful I am sure they will be only too pleased to help. When they have given you their diaries, sit down with someone and talk them through. What has surprised you about the way people eat? Is there anything in particular that scares you? How does this way of eating compare to the way you eat? The aim of this task is to help you to get a concept of what normal eating is so that you know what you are aiming for.

PLANNING YOUR 'ROAD' TO CHANGING YOUR EATING HABITS
At this stage you will be aware of various things about the way you eat now that are not part of normal eating and therefore need to change. Earlier we looked at how to draw 'road diagrams', which start where you are now and finish where you want to be. Take some time with whoever is helping you to draw a road diagram for how you need your eating to change. Remember that eating is often about a sociable experience as well as nutrition! Your road plan is likely to include a mixture not just of things to do with *what* you eat, but also some things about *how* and *where* you eat. So you might have things like 'Try eating something that has cheese in it', 'Eat three meals a day' or 'Cook a meal without counting all the calories in it', as well as some things like 'Eat out at a restaurant' or 'Eat a meal with friends'. Normal eating is about enjoyment and it is as important to develop this as it is to eat a good healthy diet.

Whatever your eating disorder, you are likely to have a list of foods that for you are particularly terrifying or forbidden. This list will vary from person to person, but is likely to include foods like chocolate, cheese, cream, cakes, biscuits and ice cream. If you are working on recovery from anorexia, then the range of foods you actually do eat might be very limited, and it might be easier to write down what you *do* eat rather than what you don't. Broadening this list is very important – both in terms of your recovery and also to help avoid the physical problems that can stem from deficiencies in certain minerals and vitamins.

Facing this kind of fear is no different from facing any other. If you were scared of heights, you would not immediately put yourself in a hot air balloon over the Grand Canyon, and in the same way, you should not expect yourself to jump right in and eat the thing that scares you the most. Instead, make a list of the foods you find hard to eat, and give each one a rating of one to ten according to how scary it is. So something like low fat yoghurt might get a two (because it is dairy and therefore a bit scary, but because you know it is fairly low calorie), whereas chocolate mousse might get a ten. Add foods to your diet starting with the least scary first. You may even be able to think of less scary versions of certain foods to help you work up to achieving your aim of adding it back into your diet. So with ice cream, for example, you might start with low calorie frozen yoghurt or sorbet, and then work up gradually towards some of the really nice brands. Remember that this is also about learning to enjoy food again, so you might also want to choose foods you really like over some that you are not so bothered about.

When you decide to try eating a food again it is important to plan with someone how you are going to do this. This avoids the fear of losing control and it also ensures that you give yourself credit for what you have achieved. So if you decide to reintroduce yoghurt into your diet, plan exactly how you will do this. What type of yoghurt will it be? Will you choose it or will someone else? When will you eat it? Will it be a snack or as pudding after a meal? Will you eat it all, or only half the pot, or will someone measure some spoonfuls from a bigger pot for you so that you do not know exactly how much you ate? Plan all these things with someone for that first time. You can work on being more spontaneous once a food is back into your diet.

Once you have started eating something again, keep it up for a couple of weeks. What you are likely to find is that the 'scariness' level of that food will probably come down quite quickly. It might not come down to a zero straight away, but it will reduce as you eat it and realize that nothing terrible is going to happen as a result.

Make sure that when you are successful in these achievements you mark them somehow. Move your marker along the road plan, or make sure that you tell whoever is supporting you about them. One idea is to put a sum of money into a jar every time you achieve a new aim, and then once a month you can take it out and treat yourself to something as a reward. You are working hard and fighting your fears, and that deserves some rewards.

What about weighing yourself?
It is not possible to write this chapter without tackling the tricky issue of whether or not to keep weighing yourself when working on recovery and tackling what you eat. Most sufferers feel they want to keep weighing themselves so that they know things have not got out of control. However, most people I know who have totally recovered from an eating disorder say that they do not weigh themselves, or at the very least do not do so regularly. More than that, many also say that it would be hard to weigh themselves regularly

without slipping back into the old patterns of worry and control. This doesn't mean they are not properly recovered. It simply means they are aware that they have this potential Achilles heel and that they might try to use controlling their weight as a way to handle other stresses in their life, so they avoid exposing themselves to that temptation or risk.

If weighing yourself regularly is part of your eating disorder, then the chances are that you will have to break this pattern eventually. This is particularly the case if it is something you do to try to handle anxiety (see Chapter 8). This does not mean that you lose all control, however. Many people find that asking someone like their GP to keep an eye on their weight is a good way of them knowing that it will not get out of hand, while not obsessively monitoring it themselves.

I am not saying that you will never be able to weigh yourself again. But if your own perception of what a weight means is inaccurate – for example, if in your mind any weight over a certain level has become unacceptable, even though that is very low for your height and build – then you will need to stop weighing yourself for a period until that link is broken. This is particularly the case if you know you have to allow yourself to put weight on in order to return to full health. It will be very hard for you to do this if you continue weighing yourself and never face the false rules and beliefs that you have about the target weights you have set yourself in the past. Remember that this is about recovery – about being free, about being healthy and getting your life back. Ultimately it is worth facing this fear in order to achieve those things.

Part 4

Supporting your child on the path to recovery
A section for parents

13 Information and advice for parents

'There are many stages and emotions accompanying the journey of anorexia from the viewpoint of a mother. For me there was fear, guilt, annoyance and feelings of helplessness as things moved out of control and my best efforts of listening and reassuring and advising my child, let alone my considerable and sometimes wily efforts to feed her, all seemed to fail. My love for her took on a renewed protectiveness that was ultra-sensitive to the stares and comments of others. I have never cried in private so much in my life.'

JANE (SEE CHAPTER 14 FOR MORE OF JANE'S STORY)

For most parents an eating disorder is the last thing they expect to encounter while raising their children. It may be something they have little or no experience of, and that moment when they realize something is going on is one that many parents have described as one of the worst of their life, dominated by the fear that stems from realizing something else is in control of their child's life; something that is seeking to disrupt and steal that life from them.

An eating disorder may emerge after what has already been a turbulent time for the family – perhaps following a marriage break-up or a death in the family. The 'child' in question may in fact be in their late teens or even older, and the parents may wonder what kind of influence or role they can have. Or it may be that the child is much younger and at the age where their parents are still theoretically responsible for much of their life. Whatever the situation, parents describe feeling totally overwhelmed by the impact of discovering a child has an eating disorder.

'I've just realized what is going on – what do I do now?'

This is the first stop you come to if you are on a journey through your child's eating disorder. It may be that they have confided in you about some of their problem. Perhaps more common, however, is the situation where you have suddenly become aware of what is going on. Perhaps you found something – hidden food, evidence of someone being sick, or a letter or diary. Perhaps someone else has alerted you – a schoolteacher, youth worker or friend. Or maybe you have arrived at this point because you have noticed changes in your child – not just in their eating and weight, but also in their mood and personality.

However you have got here, this is a very frightening place to be. It is important to remember that you are not alone. Many parents have been through this experience just like you. This is the step where things may seem the most frightening: where you have suddenly found something horrible lurking in a place where you least expected to find it. You may have found evidence of behaviours that horrify or even appal you. You may find it hard to believe that this is happening. And now, hardest of all, you have to decide what to do next.

The first question to ask yourself is whether you are the right person to approach your child about what is going on. Just because you are the one who made the discovery does not necessarily mean you are the best one to speak to them. It may be that there is someone else better equipped to bring up such a difficult subject with them.

If you think this may be the case, you need to think very carefully. Your actions should balance the need for confidentiality with the need for someone who can get alongside your child and help them to start the walk towards recovery. Most important is that your child does not feel betrayed in any way. Therefore, avoid telling lots of people, or anyone you think your child really wouldn't want to know about this. If you do decide to ask someone else to intervene, think carefully about how they will do it. Will they admit that you told them? Or is there someone else who already knows, whom you could talk to? Think about how things will seem to your child, and if in doubt don't talk to anyone without seeking advice.

It is important, however, that *someone* speaks to your child. An eating disorder can be a cry for help: a signal from someone who can tell you in no other way how bad they are feeling. If this signal is ignored, the person can become even more desperate.

It is also important that someone suffering from an eating disorder sees their GP and discusses it with him or her. An eating disorder can have serious effects on the physical health of the sufferer and it is important that someone is keeping an eye on these things. The GP is also often the person who will refer the sufferer for further specialist treatment if it is required. One of your aims in talking to your child should be to help him or her to take this first step towards getting some help. This is particularly important in younger children because they simply do not have the physical reserves of someone older and therefore can become very ill very quickly. A child under sixteen should not be losing weight, and if they have lost a lot of weight it is very important to get them to their GP to be checked out. The other reason this is important is because younger children have a more naive understanding of weight and calories, and therefore can stop drinking as well as eating. Obviously this can be extremely dangerous.

In confronting someone about their eating disorder, it is vital to remember how frightened they are. An eating disorder often makes someone do things they would never normally do, through the fear it instils in them. One main fear is of losing control of the eating routines that are helping them to cope with the way they are feeling. This is why discovery can provoke such a defensive reaction: there is often a great fear that once others know, this control will be taken from them. For this reason, it may be easier for the sufferer if you can avoid the issue of food and weight. Think of other signs that something is wrong: changes in their mood or personality, changes in things they do (for example, stopping favourite activities). Avoid mention of any falling standards of achievement in school work or any other area, as these may be interpreted as criticism. Your aim is to communicate to your child that you can see they are unhappy, and that you want to help them to feel better. If you mention their eating, you may risk them thinking, 'She just wants to make me fat.' Obviously you cannot avoid the topic altogether. However, if your first focus is not on eating this may help you to start a conversation without being shouted out of the room.

Remember while you are chatting to your child that to a sufferer an eating disorder is like a battle. They are aware that they are fighting against the illness, or against their own fears, and they are afraid that instead of helping them in this fight, anyone else who gets involved will just end up as yet another enemy to fight against, trying to make them eat and taking control from them. The best thing you can do for them, therefore, is to show clearly that you are on their side. Try to talk as little as possible, and listen to them. Resist the temptation to correct them or contradict them. For example, if they say, 'I am just so fat and I can't bear it,' rather than responding, 'But you're not fat – you could actually do with putting a bit of weight on' (you can see how this might terrify someone who fears your taking control from them and making them eat), try to respond in a way that shows them real empathy, while also showing that you disagree with them. Perhaps say something like, 'I can see that you feel really fat and that it makes you feel awful. It's obviously something that is making you feel really desperate. I don't think you are fat at all, but I'm so sorry you feel terrible. Perhaps if we work together we can help you to not feel so bad.' Emphasize the teamwork aspect rather than saying things like 'I can help you...' or 'I am going to...'. This avoids creating a fear that you will take control and it emphasizes the sufferer's own role in controlling what will happen to them.

Don't be afraid to show how you feel and to admit that this scares you as well. You do not have to pretend you have all the answers. The most valuable thing you can do is to show them that you understand how they feel, and that you will be alongside them and work together with them to try to help them to find a way out of the nightmare they have found themselves in.

Some helpful dos and don'ts

Do

- Empathize with them – be clear that you understand how they feel.

- Let them correct you if they feel you have not quite understood.

- Let them talk.

- Try to focus on how they are feeling, *not* on what they are or are not eating.

- Help to find a way for them to see their GP (perhaps it would help if you made the appointment or went with them – or even if you spoke for them).

- Emphasize that you are in this with them and that you will work with them to help them to feel better and happier.

- Avoid focusing on food and weight too much. For example, make sure you talk about recovery in terms of how they are feeling and how they are coping with their life rather than in terms of putting on weight.

Don't

- Make decisions for them – you can make suggestions, but the decision *must* come from them.

- Issue ultimatums (for example, 'If you don't go to the doctor I will tell your teachers/school/friends what is going on').

- Tell lots of people unnecessarily.

- Use emotional blackmail (for example, 'Don't you realize what this is doing to me?').

- Get caught up in endless arguments about issues surrounding food and weight – for example, whether they are or are not fat, whether eating certain foods would or would not make them fat. It is pointless and will probably result in both of you feeling frustrated, upset and fed up.

'What do I do if they refuse to admit there is a problem?'

Unfortunately the nature of an eating disorder makes it very difficult for a sufferer to admit what is going on. They may fear losing control, or be ashamed of what they are doing. Or they may not have admitted to themselves that they need help. If this is the case, then you have probably experienced some very defensive, angry and possibly rude or even violent reactions to your attempts to talk about what is happening. Please be reassured that this is often triggered by fear and is not part of your child's 'real' character. Dealing with this situation is hard and you will probably find you go through various stages. At first you may not be interested in *why* they are feeling this way, but just want some advice on how to get past this and get them to accept some help. Later on you might want to find out more about why they do feel like this.

Reasons for not admitting there is a problem

There is many reasons why your child might not be admitting to you that there is a problem. Whatever the reason is, though, it is unlikely that they are aware of it, particularly if their reaction is strong and very defensive or even abusive. The power of their feelings and reaction probably scares and shocks them as much as it does you.

If your child is in the relatively early stages of the eating disorder, they genuinely may not think there is a problem. Anorexia in particular is a 'solution' to a problem. It helps the sufferer to feel more confident, and to feel that they are in control of their life. They may have got some positive feedback from friends at school about their weight loss, and are probably enjoying the good feelings that come from that. Being in this early state of starvation also leads the body to release chemicals that can promote a feeling of well-being. These things may mean that your child is actually feeling quite good for the first time in ages. Then in you come trying to tell them they have a problem! Of course, this is not to say there are no negative sides to what they are doing. However, anorexia is very good at shielding people's eyes so that they only see the good things about it. It may be that your child is simply not admitting that there is a problem.

As anorexia develops, the negative sides to it do become clearer. The sufferer starts to feel physically much worse, and negative side-effects become more numerous. The restrictions anorexia places over their life might mean that they start to become aware that rather than them being in control, their fears of gaining weight and eating normally actually control them. In short, they may be struggling with the fear that in reality they are trapped.

This leads to two main effects as they struggle to cope with this new understanding of where they are. The first is denial, where they simply refuse to accept that this is where they are. This is a simple defence mechanism and is understandable for someone who has no idea how to cope with where they have found themselves. The second effect is that this fear becomes a very powerful force. They become terrified that if they admit what is going on, someone else will take over control and make them eat – which is the one thing they are most afraid of. This means that a lot of their reaction to your gentle questions stems from fear – which can explain why they are often so behaving out of character.

Another possible (and important) reason why they will not admit to you what is going on is that you may not be the best person to approach them. Think about what your relationship with them is usually like. Would you say that you are generally close and able to talk about how they are feeling? Are they able to be honest and open with you? You are asking them to talk with you about the most deeply emotional thing in their life so far. If they have not chosen to share less significant things with you, then it is possible that they simply do not feel able to share this with you now.

When this is the case, it is a very difficult thing for a parent to admit; parents feel a desperate need to help their children and to comfort them. However, the simple truth is that sometimes parents are in the worst possible position to take the first step in helping their children when they are suffering with anorexia. You may have to accept that it is not possible for you to take this action and move on to thinking about who would be in a better position to talk to them.

The stages of recovery

Recovery from an eating disorder requires a lot of changes in behaviour, as well as some really hard challenges to the way the person thinks about and sees the world. In any decision involving these kinds of changes, there are three stages that the person goes through. Understanding these will help you to help your child move on. Perhaps you can remember making a decision to change some aspect of your behaviour, such as to give up smoking or to try to keep your desk tidier at work. Can you remember going through the following stages as you made that decision?

1. *Pre-contemplation:* This is the stage before the person has even begun to think about changing. In their mind the behaviour has no problems associated with it and is entirely reasonable. They see no reason to want to change it in any way.

2. *Contemplation:* Moving into this stage, the person is beginning to think about the pros and cons of their behaviour. This is a stage of many mixed feelings. On the one hand they see the benefits of carrying on with the behaviour, but on the other they can see potential problems with it.

3. *Action:* This stage begins when it is realized that the costs of a behaviour outweigh the benefits. A decision is therefore made to start to change.

When you remember your own decision, you may find that you went through some of these stages several times. It isn't just a one-way process. Sometimes things that happen will push us backwards or forwards and change the way we are thinking about our behaviour. Other demands on us, such as a lack of time to look properly at positive and negative things, may mean that we are not able to move on. Alternatively, we may simply not want to move on from where we are.

GETTING SOMEONE TO THINK ABOUT THEIR BEHAVIOUR

When you talk with your child, it is first of all important to understand which stage they are at. If you approach someone who is still in a pre-contemplative stage and use a very confrontational style with them (for example, 'Don't you know that if you carry on like this you will have to drop out of school?'), all you will get is a very defensive and hostile response. The more you push, the more they will be resistant to change. This is the image of the stubborn donkey being pushed to move. The more you push, the more it digs in its heels. At this stage the sufferer has not even begun to think about changing what they are doing. The last thing they need is to be hassled about it. It is simply the wrong time to be presenting what seem to you to be very valid and important points to consider.

On the other hand, if you can be non-confrontational, listening to them and showing that you do understand how they are feeling, you will get a very different response. You can also help them to move on to a contemplative stage by gently making sure they have thought about the impact that their eating disorder might have on them. People suffering with an eating disorder tend to be very blinkered in their thinking. They often think just a few weeks ahead, or even only up to 'when I have lost those few pounds'. You can encourage them to think further into the future by asking simple questions about what their ambitions and plans are. Encourage them to think about how their eating disorder might influence their future (for example, in terms of their chances of managing at university or college or in their workplace). Make sure that you do this in a non-confrontational way, though, and if you feel yourself becoming frustrated or angry, or if they begin to seem defensive, then change the subject. Bit by bit like this you can encourage them to begin to think about their behaviour, and to weigh up its pros and cons.

Remember, therefore, that the first stage of beginning to try to help motivate someone to want to change is to understand where they are. Make time to talk to the person you are caring for. Do you understand how it feels to be in their shoes? If there are questions you need to ask, then ask them. Often sufferers talk with relief about finally having found 'someone who listens', so do take the time to do this. Make sure they know this is what you want to do: that there is no other motive rather than to be able to understand better how they are feeling. Remember that the decision to change is one only they can make. You cannot make it for them, no matter how impressive or convincing your arguments. If you want to be supportive to them, the best way you can do this is by understanding them, and by helping them to have all they need to make the right decision themselves. Then, and only then, can you begin to ask questions that might help them to be able to think more about whether or not they wish to change their behaviour and move on to work at recovery.

MOVING ON

The signs that your child is moving on will come when you see that they are starting to think about the good and bad sides of their eating disorder, rather than just blindly carrying on with it without any particular thought. It is also a stage when the potential impact of their eating disorder on things like their school work and exams might start to concern them.

At this stage it is important to help them to see that it is possible to recover fully – and to spend some time thinking with them about what recovery is. It may be helpful to put them in touch with one of the eating disorders support associations so that they can speak to someone who has recovered, or to help them to find books with stories of recovery. At this stage, it can be very tempting for you to try to push them away from the eating disorder and towards what seems to you to be so obvious. However, it is important that they are able to make up their own mind. Remember that to them their eating disorder is not *all* bad. Although there may be some negative sides to it, they are prepared to put up with those for the time being in order to benefit (as they see it) from the more positive things.

One exercise that is really useful to help you to understand things from a sufferer's point of view, as well as helping them to weigh things up in a balanced way, is the one found at the end of Chapter 5. If you do work through this exercise with your child, be very wise about how you approach it. It is not a tool designed to get them to change their mind and agree with you. It is actually about helping them to think through the real impact an eating disorder is likely to have – now and in the future. It is also a great way of helping you to understand more about what they get out of the eating disorder that is positive and why they are so resistant to getting help. Be careful, though! You may find it very tempting to point out the negatives, but do try to let them work these out as much as possible, and try very hard to understand some of the positive sides of it for them. If you are finding this really hard, it is often best to admit to them that you are somewhat biased. Use this as an opportunity to explain that you really do want to work to understand better how they are feeling. It may be that they do not really know either why the eating disorder is so attractive to them, and working through this exercise is a helpful way to get them thinking about this.

Hopefully, once you have been able to work through this exercise, your child will at least be starting to think more about their options. They may even have come to a place where they are starting to see that the eating disorder might not be such a good long-term solution to their problems. This should lead to a greater willingness to seek some help.

Sometimes, however, people suffering with eating disorders – particularly anorexia – work through these exercises but still feel very defensive and refuse to admit there is a problem. This can be very tricky to handle, and a good professional counsellor or psychologist would be specifically trained in helping them to move through this stage. But if you are having to deal with it, the main thing again is to avoid any form of confrontation. This is often easier said than done and you may find that most of your conversations do end up in confrontation. Often this is a sign that frustration and anger are being expressed. It may be that by trying to manipulate conversations with you into arguments 'for' (them) and 'against' (you) anorexia, they are actually starting to find themselves forced to admit that there are some sides of anorexia that are not wholly positive.

Always try to reflect back to them what it seems they are feeling. This is positive for two reasons: first, because they may not actually realize what they are feeling and secondly because it demonstrates to them that you do understand. If they react and say that you don't understand, then admit that you cannot put yourself entirely in their shoes, but that you do understand a little of what they are obviously feeling. Try to be sympathetic, and if you feel yourself starting to get frustrated, or getting drawn into a heated debate, withdraw gently but firmly from the conversation. It is quite acceptable for you to explain gently that you find these conversations very hard and that perhaps you could discuss this another time. You may, for example, find that your child tends to start these conversations at difficult times – when you are very busy or tired. Often this is their way of testing whether you really are interested in helping them, and for that reason it may be a good idea to suggest a time and place where you will be better able to discuss this – something clearly very important to them – together.

'What if my child won't even talk to me?'

It really is not unusual for parents to find that it simply isn't possible to sit down and have a conversation with their child about an eating disorder. If all your attempts end in shouting matches, denial and slammed doors, this is a time to think about less confrontational ways to open communication with them. Face-to-face conversation is potentially confrontational no matter how well you handle it and there are other more gentle ways of raising the subject and letting them know you care.

Letters, and even email, can be used very successfully and do at least reduce the risk of your getting shouted out of the room! Some parents have found it helpful to explain first in a letter or email that they won't talk about these things face to face, but they give a place where a reply letter can be left. If nothing else, a nice card to explain that you are worried, and to reassure them that you are not seeking to take control or make decisions for them, can show that you are on their side and not against them. If they are particularly hostile, you might suggest that they reply by letter, card or email in the same way rather than by talking to you about it. Some parents have found that stating in this card that they will not mention this issue 'out loud' has helped open communications.

Whatever happens, remember that you are not facing this alone. If your child is under sixteen, you can discuss what is happening with your GP, who should be able to give you further advice. Do also think about contacting the parent support lines operated by the main eating disorders charities (see page 144 for contact details).

A special note for those with younger children (under-sixteens) suffering with eating disorders

Eating disorders are always tricky to diagnose, but in younger children this can be particularly difficult. They may present with slightly strange sets of symptoms, or perhaps with the child offering other reasons for why they do not want to eat. Children may show a naivety in their understanding of nutrition, perhaps over-generalizing rules they have been told and becoming very anxious about what they should and should not eat. They also may not understand issues like calorie levels in foods, so may eat things which in normal circumstances someone with anorexia would not (for example, chocolate or full fat milk), relying on how they feel when they have eaten rather than any other knowledge.

There are also other conditions, mostly related to anxiety, that can lead to children losing their appetite but are not strictly eating disorders. Your GP's support here is essential, and it is important that she or he looks into exactly what is going on. *Any* unexplained or unplanned weight loss in a child under sixteen should be investigated, but it is important to remember that just as serious is a failure to gain the weight you would expect for that child's age/height. Young children do not have the energy and mineral stores of adults, and can therefore suffer physically much sooner as a result of an eating disorder, so do not delay in seeking support.

14 Supporting a child on the path to recovery: some real-life accounts

Jane's story

'Our journey began when our daughter was just eleven and in her final year at junior school, a lovely happy girl who loved playing with her sisters, who sang in the school choir, had oboe lessons and enjoyed sport, particularly swimming and netball. She began to struggle with her school work as the SATS exams loomed and the entrance tests to the upper school. She complained of the mounting tension and atmosphere in the classroom, feelings of stress in herself and the teachers. She felt that her friendships at school were changing, that she was being picked on. Some of the other more mature girls were telling her that to be "anyone", you had to be five stone or less. They even weighed her, and some other girls, at a party sleepover at someone's house. She started to become sad and withdrawn. We would sit and talk things over, just the two of us, and I'd reassure her that she was beautiful no matter what the media said, or her "friends" perceived. I told her she was perfect for her age and height. I knew how sensitive she was and what a strain she was under at school.

'I realized that her appetite was reducing and she was looking a bit thinner than usual. I had no idea what she weighed – we didn't use scales – and as far as I knew she ate well and was a perfectly average weight for her age and height. I was taking a packed tea in the car as a snack for her for the way home from school and she started saying she'd prefer not to have the crisps or the biscuits in her snack tea. I also noticed that she spent more time than usual on the trampoline, but although my suspicions were raised, I had to balance them with her need to "let off steam" during the exam period.

'The final straw came when, following her being one of the only pupils not chosen to take part in a school play, her hamsters died. We had bought them to give her something of her own to care for. We hoped that the hamsters she'd longed for would help her overcome her sadness. When they died within the first week she was inconsolable and blamed herself. It was very distressing to see her so broken. I took her off school for a few days. She was obviously losing weight and she could not seem to get out from under a depression. I felt so scared. I went to see the GP rehearsing what I needed to convey, along with some facts (height and weight, which I had now taken) for the supposed ten-minute slot.

'My GP was absolutely wonderful and gave me all the time I needed. She was concerned enough about the now noticeable weight loss and the change of emotions to refer her immediately to a specialist. I now wrestled with the near certainty that this was anorexia nervosa. All the "whats" and "ifs" and fears went through my mind as I lay awake at night. At times the fear felt overwhelming – especially as our daughter began to restrict even more the foods that she "could" and "couldn't" eat. This set up a number of feelings, including panic, frustration and heartache. We tried all sorts of favourite foods and incentives, and watched the little girl we loved so much lose not only the ability to eat but her sparkle, as she withdrew from life and, to put it in her words, just wanted "to disappear". It was heart-breaking.

'There was an eight-week period in which she lost one-and-a-half stone, which amounted to 30 per cent of her body weight, by the end of her second emergency hospital admission. During that time she was tube fed twenty-four hours a day for two weeks. She had shut down, refusing all food and drink, and was having "fits" if she ever broke her resolve, which rarely happened. When she was home, my husband and I had her sleep in between us in our bed each night and our other two daughters slept in sleeping bags at the foot of our bed for comfort. Our other two daughters needed extra love and support as they suffered their own emotions and worries. They needed support and reassurance that their feelings were perfectly understandable. My husband and I did our best to keep life as normal as possible for them, despite the strain and exhaustion and misery. Our youngest was frightened that her sister was going to die and she clung to me physically and emotionally, and would not let me out of her sight. Our elder daughter became very angry and just longed to get out of the house to be by herself. Life was hard, to say the least, and my husband was baffled initially by all the emotions.

'When a referral was made to a specialist unit for a three-month in-patient stay, the resulting out-of-area funding issue meant that we had to wait four weeks for a decision. During that time she was very ill and emotionally unstable. Finally the funding for her treatment was granted, and I spent an agonizing evening with her during her last night in hospital. I bathed her bony back and grieved.

'Returning from the clinic, a period of adjustment to "normal life" took place, which required a lot of courage from her and much patience, understanding and support from us. In fact we needed courage too in order to explain the situation to her school and to her friends and relatives, who felt she must be "better" now she was home, and that all that was "over and done with", which of course was far from the truth.

'She still needed professional counselling too, which took up where the clinic's counselling left off, but she was not willing to continue with this past a certain stage. We therefore agonized about whether she was right to try to move forward without counselling help, but felt that we had to go with her wishes, as they were rational, sensible and positive, even though it was a bit of a risk.

'In fact many of the practical aspects of her recovery required going at her pace and with gentle discussion when she raised issues, trying to support her emotionally and practically and with her eating. She had to follow a prescribed eating plan, which took effort for me as the cook too, but it was so helpful to her as she felt "safe" with it. We worried whether she would ever be able to eat freely again and be less rigid and anxious about food and about eating out. Gradually she decided to make some substitutions to her plan and then one or two additions, and although these were very small changes they required huge effort and some "risk" on her part, much understanding and patience on ours and much praise and encouragement too.

'It proved to be the start of a gradual change in her attitude towards food and then to her eating pattern generally, which also relaxed more. So too did much of her former harsh self-perception as we encouraged her with new skills and pursuits, and she saw success in her preferred subjects and hobbies at school.

'Eventually she gave up trying to plot and plan her daily food quota as life became not only more pleasurable again but also full and busy, with purpose and achievement. She began to let go of the remaining grip anorexia had on her and declare that she just wanted to be free.

'Her recovery has been rapid, though by no means easy for her or for us. She has demonstrated remarkable courage. Life is good again for her, and she has a new-found inner strength and maturity. But meanwhile we have coped with situations and emotions that I would never have imagined.'

JANE

Paula's story

'I knew something was wrong. I had a permanently sick feeling in my stomach, which started the moment I woke up in the morning and stayed until the small hours of the following morning. My husband didn't seem concerned, and my mother just thought my daughter was going through a teenage phase and was worrying about her shape and what she ate like all her friends were. She made her own breakfast, like many fifteen-year-olds do, but I rarely saw her eat it. She took a packed lunch, which I made up the night before. I realized I didn't really know how much she was eating. It obviously wasn't enough; she had lost weight and she looked so thin and pale in her baggy jumper. Our evening meals were the worst, a nightmare really. She watched over my every move when I was cooking, complaining or telling me what to do, what not to put in. Usually she said she wasn't eating it and when we managed to persuade her to sit at the table she got angry, hysterical even.

'My other children were really frightened. Her behaviour was terrible most of the time. I'd never seen her like it before, and trying to explain it to people was so difficult because you could see they were thinking I was exaggerating. Even my GP was unsympathetic and said he couldn't do anything unless she wanted to see him, which she flatly refused to do. We noticed some scratches and cuts on her arm, and it was a huge shock to realize that she was harming herself. It also upset me to find the sandwiches I had packed for her lunch hidden in her waste bin in her room. I have never cried so much in all my life. The daughter I loved, hurting and hitting out at us all, and me feeling useless and powerless to help her.

'I began to be really vigilant and to read as much as I could about eating disorders. It upset me to realize that she was obviously doing so many of the things listed, such as going to the bathroom straight after tea, but it was comforting to know that this was a definite illness and that I was not alone. Talking to people who have been through this themselves, who just listened to me and answered all my questions, helped me to manage things at home differently and was an answer to prayer. It was so important for me to be able to look at ways together with them that I could approach my daughter and the GP. But there were also times when I felt completely exhausted and that no one knew what was going on or how I was feeling.

'I went to my GP alone for a chat, really to see how the surgery could approach our daughter. We had tried writing her a letter telling her how much we loved her and wanted to support her through what must be a very frightening time of her life and that we realized she was sad and depressed and we wanted to help her. My doctor suggested that maybe she would see a new doctor, a lady doctor, and that perhaps by focusing on our daughter's depression and not on her eating disorder she might want to go to the surgery.

'It was the way in, because although she was trying to deny that she had an eating disorder, she was ready to receive some support for feeling so sad and out of control. Having her own doctor was also important for her in terms of confidentiality and independence. I was so relieved that someone was looking after her medically and that hopefully when the time was right her GP would bring the conversation round to the root of the problem. The GP brought in the surgery's dietician after a while, to show our daughter how certain foods can help lift depression and to subtly look to her diet, but it didn't help her rigid regime at home. She seemed to be eating fewer and fewer types of food and rowing with us all the time over food and her life generally. It was awful having to wait and not quiz her every time she came back from a doctor's appointment, but eventually she told me that she had been given an appointment with a specialist and asked if I would go along.

'I really set my hopes on the consultant, as she was a specialist in eating disorders. She counselled our daughter weekly for four months, and saw us as a family in order to help us all understand anorexia and to help us help our daughter. She put her on a special diet, which she explained would first stabilize her weight and then give her a very small one pound a week gain. Our daughter was horrified at first, but when she realized that it was either this or hospital, she agreed to try. The consultant was really good, and counselled her with a real interest in her problems and anxieties. It was wonderful to see, and to have another authority figure she could listen to, someone we relied on.

'After the four months, the consultant felt that our daughter would benefit from seeing the team at the local child and adolescent unit and maybe taking some of her lunchtime meals there. She had made a seven-pound weight gain, but it was now felt that a step towards a less structured diet and eating with others would help her. We went weekly to start with and each time her weight was checked and her blood pressure was recorded. The nurses and the psychologist helped to keep her motivated and on track. They also provided advice for me, and family therapy for all of us, which was good but exhausting.

'We didn't always see progress and there were weeks when her weight dropped. Often she threw tantrums when being weighed or counselled. It was embarrassing, but the staff were clearly used to it and I found it reassuring to know that they understood that this was happening at home. They said I could ring them any time her behaviour got too much for me, and I did often ring them, which was so helpful. There was a time when she started to refuse some of the items on the dietician's food plan for her. I think it was when she was given some choice, for example between potato and rice, and this choice she found really hard. We had to encourage her and remind her how well she was doing, which was difficult because she flew into rages with us and with her sisters whenever we said anything, and her self-harming became more frequent.

'We managed to struggle on over the difficult stage, largely I think because she really didn't want to be admitted to the unit as an in-patient and miss going to school and seeing her friends. This was the best motivation of all – seeing what the anorexia was taking away from her, and if she wasn't careful her schooling and her future too. We decided to get extra private counselling help to support the work of the unit. This turned out to be very useful to her, as she was able to pour out all the negative feelings she had about the unit and her weight gaining programme to the counsellor and to believe that it was she who was deciding to try to get better and not because she was ordered to by the unit.

'It took months and months, but little by little we saw her relax a bit about eating with us as a family and start to think more positively about herself and what she wanted to do with her life. Eventually she began to realize that anorexia was not her friend after all and that in order to live her life she had to learn new ways of coping without it. I guess in many ways that was the start of her moving towards recovery.'

PAULA

Further Support

For further help or support, contact one of the two national eating disorders charities:

Anorexia & Bulimia Care (ABC) is the national Christian charity working with all who suffer because of eating disorders. It is able to offer help and support, as well as the chance to have a befriender – someone who has had experience of recovery from an eating disorder and can support someone else who is still struggling towards recovery. ABC has a specific helpline for parents or those concerned about younger teens and children called ACHE (Anorexic Children, Help and Encouragement).

Website: www.anorexiabulimiacare.co.uk
Tel: 01462 423 351
Email: help@anorexiabulimiacare.co.uk
Helpline for ACHE: 01934 710 336 or email
ache@anorexiabulimiacare.co.uk

BEAT (previously the Eating Disorders Association) is the biggest organization in the UK working with eating disorders. It is an organization offering information and help, as well as running support groups and providing various resources.

Website: www.b-eat.co.uk
Tel: 0845 634 1414
Email: helpmail@edauk.com
Helpline for young people: 0845 634 7650 (text on 07786 201 820) or email help@b-eat.co.uk or fyp@b-eat.co.uk